Public internet access
in libraries and
information services

Public internet access in libraries and information services

Paul Sturges

facet publishing

© Paul Sturges 2002

Published by
Facet Publishing
7 Ridgmount Street
London WC1E 7AE

Facet Publishing (formerly Library Association Publishing) is wholly owned by CILIP: the Chartered Institute of Library and Information Professionals.

First published 2002

British Library Cataloguing in Publication Data

A catalogue record for this book is available from the British Library.

ISBN 1-85604-425-4

Typeset from author's disk in 11/14 Elegant Garamond and Humanist by Facet Publishing.
Printed and made in Great Britain by MPG Books Ltd, Bodmin, Cornwall.

Contents

Acknowledgements

I owe to Giuseppe Vitiello (formerly of the Council of Europe) the opportunity to begin some research in the autumn of 1997 that eventually led to the writing of this book. Like many others who have worked with him, I have been inspired by his knowledge and enthusiasm and feel proud to consider him a friend as well as a colleague. Subsequently I have also accumulated debts of gratitude to many other Council of Europe staff, consultants and members of national delegations, for their insights and professional good fellowship. It has always been a pleasure to be associated with the Council of Europe. It may not have the power or finances of its near namesake the European Commission, but it is a fertile seedbed of policy ideas.

Over the years information professionals working for many libraries and other institutions have helped me in many different ways. I would risk missing names if I tried to list them all. However, I must give particular mention to Elizabeth Melrose of North Yorkshire County Library and her colleagues, Bryan Berryman, George Capel, Jeremy Grayson, Iris Maynard, Helen Parsons, Chris Pearson, Nigel Prince, Angie Simpson and Sarah Stocks, who gave me the benefit of their experience during a delightful day in Northallerton.

Thanks also to my expert readers, Andy Bissett, Marigold Cleeve, Elizabeth Orna and Goff Sargent, who helped me identify errors and weaknesses in my text, but who are in no way responsible for any inadequacies in the finished book. I am particularly grateful to Hazel Grant of Bird and Bird, for running her professional eye over Chapter 4 'The law and the internet'. The staff of Library Association Publishing have been a great support, particularly Helen Vaux, who commissioned the book, and Helen Carley, who saw it through part of its gestation period (at the same time as she was expecting her own baby). Finally, my wife Claire has helped in many different ways, not least in reading the text before its final revision.

Introduction

This is a book designed to help you, as an information professional, to provide public access to the internet in a way that will bring confidence to everyone concerned. Before starting I am going to define and discuss the main concepts that I use. You can skip this section if you want to get on with what the book actually says, but if you do that it will still be here for you to refer back to if you need to. The definitions are just about how and why I use the main terms. I am not going to use a lot of space comparing what the dictionaries say, and I am not too worried about the theoretical coherence of the definitions. Not surprisingly, the list starts with 'information'. I have sometimes felt like screaming when forced to read or listen to yet another definition of information and you may feel the same. But just because people use it in so very many different ways, I need to say what I mean when I use it (and like everyone else, I use it all the time). For an accessible survey of other people's definitions you could look at an article by Bawden (2001).

Definitions

Information

I define information as facts and ideas communicated. For me, the 'facts' part of this can cover everything from data in raw and processed forms, right through to any kind of material that describes and provides detail on one subject or another. The 'ideas' part includes the whole range from philosophy, theories and inventions, through to artistic and cultural creations. This makes it possible to include material designed to amuse or entertain. This may seem to stretch the definition too far, but actually it enables us to look at what people want as a whole, without artificially separating the serious from the frivolous. By 'communicated' I really mean that it is put in absolutely any kind of form, such as a statement made in conversation, a song, a book, a newspaper article, a photograph or painting, a CD, or a web page, so that it can be communicated from one person to another. Information packages of these kinds are frequently referred to as 'content', and that is a term that I also use in this book. My definition of information might well horrify theorists, but it is intended to be all-inclusive and reflect everything that information can mean in the real world.

Information professional

By this I mean people who work with information as intermediaries. Information workers might be a better alternative term in some ways, but it carries an implication of 'workers with the hand' as opposed to 'workers with the mind' and perhaps that is unhelpful. I use the term to include librarians, information scientists, and people who work in information and advice centres, as well as archivists, records managers and museum curators. It includes both salaried professionals in the public service and those who work for profit as consultants and brokers. I also intend it to include people who do information work as unpaid volunteers, when that seems convenient. To be absolutely logical, the definition should probably include people such as publishers, journalists, broadcasters and creators of content for electronic services. That is not really a problem, because the book deals with topics that are relevant to them too. The point of using the term information professionals is that it includes rather than excludes, and enables me to write for just about everyone who is likely to find this book useful. However, I do see more of a distinction between information professionals and those in the information technology and information systems sectors. Information technology is driven by a combination of technical innovation and hard commercial reasoning, and while information systems experts always stress that they create systems for people, it often seems that they create technology-centred systems to which people have to accommodate themselves. To me the work of the information professional is distinguished by an ethic of service to people, but professionals providing information technology services, and systems experts working on the human–computer interface ought to find this book helpful.

Information institution

This is a clumsy term which I use to include libraries, information centres, learning and resource centres, museums, archives and records management centres, and other providers of information services to all, or a segment of, the public. Usually these are in the public sector as far as finance is concerned. Some people might think that a term like 'knowledge institutions' would be preferable, but to me that opens up more problems than it solves. Indeed, lumping all these types of institution in one category, whatever you call it, might seem like a mistake. But what they have in common is that they are all seeking to inform, educate and sometimes entertain through provision of information content in some form. More to the point, for the purposes of this book, is that all of them, actually or potentially, provide public access to the internet. This makes it possible to write in general terms about important aspects of what they do.

Access

In this book I use access in the sense of access to information through technology. There are many other variations on the way the term is used and it is an important word way beyond the limits of the information world. For instance, it carries with it powerful implications of democracy and social inclusion. A particularly important use is in referring to people's ability to obtain social benefits of all kinds. This is relevant because information in this sense is either just another social benefit, or maybe even the key social benefit in that it can unlock other benefits (welfare payments, medical care, education etc.). Access is also used a great deal in the narrower sense of 'access to technology'. This usually means actually owning the equipment (computers and peripherals) or having it provided for you, for instance in your office. It is sometimes extended to mean having the skills to use technology to good effect. Although this book often refers to these aspects of access, access to technology is not the main concern. It is access to what lies behind the technology, or is available through the technology, that I shall be talking about. Today this means information from the internet, though in the future it will probably mean some information system or medium that is well nigh impossible for the average person to imagine at present.

Public access

By adding 'public' to 'access', I mean shared availability of technology so that people can get information. In practical terms this generally means computers and networked terminals provided by public information institutions such as libraries, information centres, archives and museums for use by anyone who needs them. There is also public access at kiosks in places like railway stations and post offices, or even in the street at internet terminals of the kind that have been provided in Dutch and Swiss cities. Another variant is facilities like the park bench in Bury St Edmunds, England, that is provided with ports so that people can plug in their laptops and use them in the open air. Private access to technology is not possible for everyone, and publicly available networked terminals are important because they can make sure that the gaps left by domestic and business access are filled. Some of these gaps are filled by private sector institutions like internet cafés. They provide an important service, but their purpose is to provide a service that will fill gaps in private provision so as to make, or improve, profits. Public access, in the sense in which I use it, is much more than just filling gaps. Public information institutions provide shared technology, just as they have always provided shared information resources, to ensure that everyone can get the fullest and most up-to-date information available. What I regard as true public access is this kind of access to technology provided as part of a full range of information services. It is provided regardless of whether people have technology or information resources at home or in their offices, and it is managed by professionals so that it can be used to the best effect.

Assurance

The word assurance is used in this book because I believe that public access needs to be managed, and is not just about providing facilities and leaving users to deal with them as best they can. In particular, it is about giving users some reason to be confident of the quality of what is offered. Access to information is a valuable thing in its own right, but if it comes with assurance that the system and the information obtainable through it are good, that is even better. Dictionary definitions of assurance mention certainty, confidence, guarantees and warranties, commitment, indemnity and insurance against bad outcomes. An assurance is a positive declaration that something is true. These are the kinds of terms that it should be possible to use when describing the services that we provide to the public. They imply other values such as safety, fairness and accountability. There has been a great deal of work on developing quality assurance mechanisms for the information and library sector, and this book brings a broad version of the assurance concept to provision of public access to the internet. What I suggest is that being able to offer the public an assurance that the information service that they are getting is of good quality depends on adopting clear and effective policies.

Information policy

Usually when people talk about information policy they are thinking of international organizations and governments dealing with information issues at global, regional and national levels. However, this book is about information policy at a much more everyday level – policy in individual institutions. Institutions need to have a clear set of values, to identify aims and objectives and to develop a strong policy-making process. This process should result in clear statements of what the institution is seeking to do and how it intends to go about achieving its aims. These statements guide the people who work in the institution, but they also need to be put in suitable form for presentation to users. The statements to users form a kind of contract setting out what all the people involved should be able to expect from each other. In general terms the values of information services are pretty clear, but the aims and objectives of your own particular service are something that has to be thrashed out within your institution. No one can set out standard aims and objectives for you, but guidance on how to make policy can be very useful. Fortunately there is an excellent book by Orna (1999) on making information policies, which I can strongly recommend to you. It does, however, leave plenty of scope for other books, like this one, on specific aspects of policy making.

What this book does

This book is designed to help you form policy on all aspects of public internet access in your own institution. Things are changing so fast in the information world that this is a time when policy guidance is particularly important. Computer technology and modern telecommunications are being brought together in a bewildering variety of ways, but for information professionals the internet is the main concern. At present it complements information services in the form of print, or mass media such as radio and TV. In the fairly near future it seems possible that the internet or, more likely, a successor technology will dominate information provision so completely that the more familiar forms may become much less relevant. That worry is there for the medium and the long term but for the short term (the next few months and the next few years) dealing with the internet itself is the issue. There are all kinds of anxieties, public and professional, about the information and communication that the internet brings, and the way in which it brings them. Policies that help in coping with change are very necessary.

This is not a theoretical book: it is concerned with helping you to develop policies that will work in practice. To do that I have to provide a certain amount of background information, but that does not mean there is any need to be comprehensive. There are plenty of other sources that deal with topics such as, for instance, the full intricacies of the debate on internet filtering, or all the conceivably relevant aspects of the law on copyright. I will provide details of plenty of sources of help, but I do not believe that it is necessary to give you every reference or URL, or to name every useful organization. An academic study of the topic might need to deal with all this, but I will try to give you what I think you can use, and not a lot more. I hope that after using the book you will feel able to make a confident contribution to preparing and drawing up policy documents for your institution. I believe that in doing so you will create confidence between you, your funders, your colleagues, the people who use your services and anyone else, such as politicians and campaigners, with an interest in information provision issues.

Who this book is for and why

As I have suggested in the definitions provided above, I have written this book for quite a wide range of potential readers. Public access to the internet is provided in different ways in all sorts of different institutions, and the intention is to provide something useful for you if you are involved in any of them. Categories of potential readers include professionals providing the following:

- full public access in libraries and information centres
- what amounts to public access in colleges and universities

- access mainly restricted to specialized purposes in schools, museums, archives and research libraries.

A word or two about each of these sectors follows so as to show how they fit.

Libraries and information centres

Libraries and information centres for the general public are a major source of public internet access. Increasingly, most libraries in developed countries are in some way 'hybrid' libraries mixing print and other media and giving some degree of public access to digital resources. If you are a librarian, you and your institution may be very clear on policy relating to print and other hard-copy resources. It is very unlikely that policy on access to digital resources is as clear, and this needs to be remedied. There are also a host of other general information and advice centres, many of them provided by local authorities and non-governmental organizations, that provide one or more terminals for public internet access and there are kiosks in public places that provide at least some limited access to websites. If you are responsible for a service of this kind, you need access policies too.

Colleges and universities

If you work as an information professional in an academic institution, you are very likely to be providing what amounts to public access, even though this is only for students, researchers and staff. Your institution provides access essentially to meet teaching and research aims and often, formally speaking, it does not permit access for other purposes. In practice a blind eye is usually turned to non-essential use, or non-essential use is permitted for the goodwill that this creates. In this way academic institutions provide many thousands of users with more or less the same kind of general public access as public libraries and information centres give to the world at large. The facilities may be in the library or learning centre, or in computer laboratories with networked machines. Computer laboratories may be available for independent study, without the equivalent of a librarian in charge, but the college or university still has a responsibility for what happens there. This calls for policy, though maybe rather different policy from that needed in the library or learning centre.

Specialized institutions

Public access terminals in research libraries (including national and special libraries), archives, museums and specialized information centres are like those in academic institutions. They are there so that users can work on the topics in which the institution specializes. In practice the institution often allows some general use. This may be even more at the discretion of you, as the professional in charge, than the general use allowed in academic institutions. However, because you need to form judgements on what sorts of access are relevant or not, and just how much non-relevant access might be acceptable, you also need to work on policy. The most difficult area of all falls into this 'specialized' category, and this is school and other children's libraries and learning centres. It is not easy to devise a coherent policy for restricting children and young people to relevant access. More energy is likely to be required in working out just how to ensure children get the benefit that can be obtained from the internet than in any of the other sectors. If you are responsible for children's access you probably need the content of this book more than anyone else.

Others

Other potential readers include students on programmes containing modules on topics such as information management. It could also be valuable for information technology and information systems people to broaden their approach by looking more closely at the approach of the information service professions. At the end of a long list like this it is common to add 'and the general reader' just to catch anyone missed and maybe sell an extra copy or two. Unfortunately, I cannot honestly claim that there will be much for general readers here, unless they happen to have an unusually strong interest in finding out what troubles the minds of information professionals. However, politicians, campaigners and lobbyists could certainly read this with advantage, so information professionals please lend them a copy, or better still encourage them to buy one.

Who the book is not for (but who might usefully consult it)

The book is not specifically aimed at providers of internet access who do this on a totally private basis. Employers who provide access for their staff do so only so that staff can do the organization's work effectively. At the most they may allow some non-essential access for relevant study, or activities relating to a trade union or a professional association. Their policies, so long as they are legal, are their own business. The same is true of the owners and managers of internet cafés, who provide internet access strictly as a means of obtaining a profit. However, even managers from the purely private sector need to think about how they can provide assurance to their employees and clients in very much the same way as is appropriate for public institutions. Consequently I believe that private providers of internet access may also find some useful guidance here.

How this book is organized

There are three main parts to the book:

- The first (Chapters 1 and 2) deals with the problems and issues connected with public access provision for the internet. Chapter 1 sets out what the internet is and what it does, so as to put public access issues in context. Chapter 2 outlines the relevant debates on internet content and public access.
- The second (Chapters 3, 4 and 5) reviews the ethical, legal and practical background to the policy-making process. Chapter 3 shows how the debates take place in the ethical environment and provides guidance on handling questions of professional ethics. Chapter 4 provides an information professional's view of relevant law. Chapter 5 sets out the scope of the management of internet access and the types of policy issue that are involved
- The third (Chapter 6 and Appendices) is a systematic guide to policy making in practice, supported by the documents in the Appendices and the references in the Reading List and List of Selected Websites.

References

Bawden, D. (2001) The shifting terminologies of information, *Aslib Proceedings*, **53** (3), 93–8.

Orna, E. (1999) *Practical information policies*, Aldershot, Gower.

1
Public access to information on the internet

Although the internet has only been in place in its current form for a short time, it has expanded so fast and it has been talked about so much that it seems like something that has been around forever. I realized how much a part of the everyday world it had become at a reception a couple of years ago. I was introduced to a genteel elderly lady and her opening remark was not about the weather or the hostess's canapés, but 'Tell me, what web browser do you recommend?' Because the internet has become taken for granted to such an extent, it is worth reminding ourselves just what it is and how it came to be.

This chapter is organized in the following way: first I will look at the key features of the internet that matter in relation to access, then I will look at the way in which people gain access to the internet and its content, before dealing with public provision of access facilities. Finally I will talk about what is involved in the management of public internet access.

The internet
What is the internet?

To understand internet access we need at least a basic understanding of what the internet actually is in practical terms. Putting aside all considerations of content, or scientific, social and economic significance, essentially the internet is a set of computer networks linked by software protocols called TCP/IP (Transmission Control Protocol/Internet Protocol). The protocols allow the computers within a network to communicate with each other and with other computers in other networks, using a common address system.

Underlying this there is an infrastructure that consists basically of routers (computers that receive and move packets of data onwards to where they are addressed), hosts (which hold programs and data) and pipes (the telecommunications links through which the data passes). The pipes are largely provided by telecommunications companies and the hosts and routers tend to be owned by governments and private organizations. All of this physical infrastructure is made to work as one system by a complex system of contracts and payment arrangements between the owners of the routers, hosts and pipes. However, this is all effectively invisible to the user, who mainly cares about questions of access and content.

The internet as we know it originates in the American defence network ARPANET set up in the 1960s. This was expanded by linking with mainly academic networks, such as Britain's JANET (Joint Academic Network), in the 1970s. ARPANET began to move away from its purely defence/research orientation in the late 1970s, with Usenet newsgroups being set up for users to discuss topics of almost any kind. The term internet does not seem to have been used until 1982 and it was soon after this that TCP/IP was introduced to give the network its essential character. The most significant year from our point of view was probably 1991, with two enormously important developments:

- The first was the creation of the world wide web (WWW, or just the web).
- The second was the lifting of restrictions on commercial use of the internet.

The web

The web is the facility that enables internet users to point and click at their screen and move seamlessly between parts of a website or between different websites just as if they were all the pages of a book, or piles of books, on top of a single desk. The location of each document on the web is specified precisely by its Uniform Resource Locator (URL) and the document is delivered to the user's browser using Hyper Text Transmission Protocol (HTTP). The browser, or one of a number of ancillary programs, or plug-ins, is able to display the document, provided it is written in a standard file format, usually Hyper Text Mark-up Language (HTML). This allows users to access documents either if they know the URL, or if the creators of a website have deliberately provided hypertext links to those documents. It is the smoothness with which this works that makes internet content easily accessible to people who are not necessarily comfortable using computer software packages. So important for the average user is the web that they very often forget all the non-web communication that goes off on the internet and all the non-hypertext resources that are also available to the more resourceful user. Because the web makes the internet attractive to non-technically-minded users, its existence created a break-through in the number of users and the volume of content created to cater for a multitude of interests. In turn, this has proved absolutely irresistible to commercial organizations looking for new sales and marketing opportunities.

Commercialization

During the 1990s, the internet very quickly became a genuinely significant commercial medium. The volume and range of commodities traded via the internet expanded swiftly and it is now possible electronically to order and pay for most types of goods, to obtain services and to conduct investment and other financial transactions. Governments have actively contributed to the shift towards a more commercial internet ethos. The influential 1994 report of the High-Level Group on the Information Society (the Bangemann Report) treated the electronic environment as a sphere in which Europe needed to compete effectively with the USA, and should do so with a completely commercial ethos.

> The Group is convinced that technological progress and the evolution of the market mean that Europe must make a break from policies based on principles which belong to a time before the advent of the information revolution. The key issue for the emergence of new markets is the need for a new regulatory environment allowing full competition. This will be a prerequisite for mobilising the private capital necessary for innovation, growth and development.
>
> (Bangemann, 1994)

Business in Europe has responded to this, but the great American corporations still set the pace. Mergers, like that of America Online and Time Warner, completed in January 2001, create internet-oriented media corporations capable of investment on just about any scale the future might require. However, the dot.com stock market boom in the shares of internet-based companies in the second half of 2000 grossly over-valued the growth of internet commerce, at least in the short term. For instance, the internet service provider Freeserve was for a short while more heavily capitalized than industrial giants such as Rolls-Royce. Nevertheless, the public face of the internet is now highly commercial and e-business has very quickly come to be the highest profile aspect of internet activity. In fact it is sometimes worth reminding ourselves that there is still an immense volume of non-commercial activity on the internet.

Access to the internet

Getting access

Originally, the way an individual user obtained access to the internet was as a member of an organization, typically a government body or a university, that had computers linked to a network within the internet. Nowadays, of course, there are great numbers of access providers that sell internet access to home and commercial users. What they offer includes a variety of arrangements ranging from simple dial-up accounts for home users and small businesses using a modem to connect their computers to the internet via telephone lines, ISDN and broadband connections; to leased lines dedicated to internet use; and to services that go beyond access as such, to include web hosting and design. The important thing for us to remember is that all of this, though we refer to it as public access, is still in the most important sense private access. You obtain it through your employment or enrolment at an educational institution, or because you pay to connect your own computer. In fact, enormous numbers of people have both of these kinds of what is essentially private access to the internet.

The number of networks linked to the internet is so large and is growing so fast that it is more or less impossible to estimate how many there are, let alone to know how many computers there are attached to these networks, or to estimate the number of people who have access (except in round millions). It is also important to remember that there are many private networks of companies and other institutions that also use TCP/IP, many of which will have some sort of gateway into the internet, but which are not supposed to be accessible from outside. Despite this, there are two extremely important things that you obtain when you get access to the internet:

- Access to the contents of computers all over the world. Servers, that is computers permanently connected to the internet (as opposed to linked up occasionally when the user wants to make specific use of it), are freely accessible to users other than their owner or members of the owner's organization. Although the data that they supply is typically read-only, or even password controlled, it is nevertheless a public resource.
- The sense that the internet is all one system. The common protocols and addressing systems allow all those computers to be accessed without the user having to make completely fresh connections to each, or to use different software systems.

The internet as a library

Because of the sense that the internet is one entity, and because the computers linked to it hold a vast wealth of information, it is quite common to hear the internet referred to as a kind of library, accessible for consultation by any internet user. While it is not necessarily a good idea to take the library analogy too literally, asking why the internet is sometimes compared with a library, and working out the ways in which this is valid and the ways in which it is misleading, is an approach worth pursuing for a while. What makes the library analogy such an obvious one is the web. Servers connected to the internet all over the world contain vast numbers of websites on just about every conceivable topic, created by everyone from Nobel prize winners and their research teams, or highly-capitalized data collection and publication services, through to enthusiastic kids passionately promoting their own favourite aspect of popular culture. Certainly you can use the internet as if it were a library. If it is current material that you want, and if your critical faculties are sufficiently developed for you to distinguish information of good quality from the rest, you can use it to excellent effect.

The difference is that libraries, even the enormous national libraries that seem to collect everything indiscriminately, are always the product of a selection process. Even if not every individual document is assessed and deliberately chosen for inclusion, the categories of material that are acquired are selected. Rather similarly, the content of archive repositories is absolutely tied to some specific source or sources of documents. Museums, by definition, only offer samples of types of object: complete access is an absurdity. That would mean designating the world and everything in it as a museum. More importantly, all of these types of information institution organize their resources and provide catalogues and other finding aids.

Rather than being like a library, the internet is much more like a great publishing industry, with anyone who chooses able to publish and the whole output offered in an open market. What appears on the internet is not selected and it is not catalogued. It is, however, browsable and the basic browsing can be done by automatic means on the users' behalf. This is possible because the software environment permits the indexing and retrieval activities of search engines. By making use of search engines, the user is able to treat the internet as if it were a library.

Search engines

Search engines are most users' first resort when information is needed, but most users (myself included) have only a pretty vague idea of how they work. We merely know that if we make a reasonably good choice of search terms, the system retrieves enormous lists of material that might be relevant. What is more, if we are lucky there is genuinely relevant material at the top of the list. However, there are difficulties. For instance, no one seems sure just how deeply the search engines do penetrate the resources of the internet. Some commentators have suggested that what is identified represents as little as 1% of the total that might be found. No information professional is likely to feel very comfortable with levels of penetration like this if searches seem to be missing vital information. However, on the other hand, searches do actually identify a bewildering number of sources and users generally seem to feel that they obtain something that satisfies their need when searching the web. No one but a total obsessive would want to have access to everything out there anyway. Anyone with access to a server can create and make available their own web pages. Many do, and it results in myriads of appalling garbage heaps, from which worthwhile material has to be distinguished somehow or other. If the search engines are locating the 'right' fraction of the available content they are doing their job effectively.

Also, the effectiveness of search engines is constantly being refined, and users now have some choice as to the type of engine that they might opt for with a particular search. Free-text search engines (like Google) can identify names of sites, or terms that occur in sites, if they are reasonably distinctive, but any ambiguous term or very common name is likely to be lost in a welter of irrelevancy. Categorized directory sites (like Yahoo! and various subject-specific search engines) are helpful in locating material that can be placed within a particular subject domain. New generations of search engines are emerging with the capacity to search much more widely and locate interesting files even in the hard disks of individuals who have made their computers available as servers so that others can access music, video and other material that they wish to exchange on a peer-to-peer (P2P) basis. Users can increasingly get the impression that the automatic searches that they initiate are tapping the whole wealth of the system, even if that may not be entirely true. One reason why it may not be entirely true arises from the activities of the commercial sector of the web. This problem will be discussed in the next chapter.

Interactivity

There is, however, another major feature which differentiates the internet from virtually all of the other information mediums that a public information service uses or provides. It is much more than just a set of information resources linked by the web: it is a truly interactive system. It offers communication facilities like e-mail, file downloading, newsgroups and chatrooms, and in offering full public access to the internet an institution has to be aware that it is granting users an autonomy of a kind that it has never offered before. This is crucial when we start to look at the problems of public access provision. The internet is not another medium like books, microforms, audio and video recordings. It simultaneously has the ability to distribute content to large numbers of people in the way broadcast media like radio and television do, while providing personal communication facilities in the same way as telecommunications media such as the telephone.

Libraries, information centres, archives and museums have no real experience of interactive services. Well-presented physical (as opposed to electronic) resources can seem as though they are interactive. They can be supported by other sources that complement and supplement them, or material can be interpreted by the institution, as museums do so well these days. When you use a book or manuscript, or examine a museum object for the knowledge that you may be able to gain from it, you are basically on your own. What you learn from it is just your interpretation and understanding. If you had the cheek you could write to, phone up or even drop in on an author, just as the women from the launderette (in the Monty Python sketch) did when they wanted to consult Jean-Paul Sartre about some point of philosophy. Most of the time, however, you cannot do much other than compare your own judgement of what something means with any criticisms of it that you can find. Most of any dialogue that takes place, takes place inside your own mind. The internet, because it offers communication facilities along with documents and other information resources, is genuinely interactive, and managing an interactive medium is an almost completely new departure for information professionals.

Public access

Public terminals

Problems or not, great numbers of libraries and other information institutions are already offering internet access to their users as a normal part of their services. In the summer of 1995 I visited a number of small and medium-sized public libraries in England with an overseas visitor. At this time higher education institutions were well on the way to providing information and communication facilities for all their staff and students using computerized systems. Schools too had introduced computers in fair numbers, though provision was very uneven. What we saw in the libraries also included plenty of computers, but at that stage there was very little evidence of coherent provision. There were OPACs, software banks, access points for local intranets, standalone computing facilities for use with word-processing and other standard software packages, and a few internet terminals. Sometimes there were four or five separate and incompatible public computer facilities in a library. Also, at precisely that point in time the UK Library and Information Commission reported that nearly half of the public libraries offering the internet were still charging users for access (Ormes and Dempsey, 1995). Since then things have changed very much indeed.

The information professions have clearly identified public internet access as a high priority and directed funding towards it as far as they have been able. There has also been government intervention on an increased scale since the British elections of 1997. This has come in the form of initiatives like Culture Online (intended to make cultural resources more accessible through the use of technology) and UK Online (to offer public access and training for the internet), both launched in March 2001. With the latter the British government plans to have 6000 free public UK Online Centres in operation in community facilities, businesses and shops by the end of 2002. All of the country's 3500 public library service points are intended to form part of this total. By mid-2001, 65% of these public library service points were already offering internet access on a total of 6351 terminals. However, these figures taken from People's Network (2001) are increasing so fast that what is printed here is merely a historical snapshot. This progress has built on what was recommended in *New library: the people's network* (Library and Information Commission, 1997). Following on from this document, the government provided large sums of money for training library staff in ICT, creating content for a library network, and developing infrastructure. Despite this progress and these plans Britain is not even an outstanding example in spreading public access. Anyone who has visited the libraries and information centres of Finland or Sweden in the last few years will know just how widespread and how enthusiastically received public access can be.

On the other hand, activity in public libraries is only part of the story. Many academic and special libraries offer a much greater mix of print and different forms of electronic access, including the internet and other digital resources. The same kind of thing is happening in record offices and museums, where electronic catalogues and virtual counterparts to the documents and artifacts are becoming quite common. There are also wholly digital or electronic libraries and/or learning centres where the only print is the computer manual (and nobody relies very much on that). This is very important but leading edge institutions are, in terms of their impact on the population as a whole, less significant than the everyday centres, like public libraries, that are to be found in every town and suburb. It is there that we can find some of the answers to what access to the internet in public institutions really means. We also need to look at internet access as a whole.

Statistics of use

Some official British figures (National Statistics, 2001) tell an interesting story. They indicate that 51% of the British adult population at the time of the survey (over 23 million people) had accessed the internet. This figure included both regular users and also those who had merely obtained occasional access. In looking at the figure it is important to remember that

British internet take-up lags behind that of many countries, and that patterns will generally differ according to where in the world we look. A closer look at the British total shows that it includes higher proportions of men than women (57% as opposed to 46%), more young than older people (82% of 16–24-year-olds as opposed to 16% of over-65s) and more people from professional households than from those of unskilled workers (72% as opposed to 23%). Also, 37% of those surveyed had accessed the internet mainly at work and, in theory, though probably not in practice, should not have made any private use of it. What this represents is a very uneven distribution of access. Turning to those who had not used the internet: 45% said that they were not interested in doing so. However the remaining 55% gave reasons that mainly fell into two categories: lack of facilities and inability to afford them on the one hand, and lack of knowledge and support on the other. The message is clear. Certain sectors of society such as women, the elderly and the less well-off are disadvantaged in terms of internet access and a large proportion of them are prevented from gaining access by lack of money and help. Almost any reading of these figures suggests in the strongest possible way the need for public access facilities.

This is the situation in a prosperous, industrialized country but in other parts of the world things are much less favourable. For instance a survey in Central and Eastern Europe (Global Internet Liberty Campaign, 2000) revealed that internet access is not at all widespread, though increasing. Poor telecommunications infrastructure is a significant reason for this, with not only home users but even non-governmental organizations dependent on dial-up connections. Proportions of homes with telephones is low, quality is often poor and there are long waiting lists for new connections. Telephone charges have increased in several countries and there are also examples of confusion arising from the process of privatization. Some governments in the region still control and censor information and have an ambivalent attitude towards the internet. Public access points are being provided in some countries (Estonia for example) and others (Hungary) have made good progress in connecting schools. Even the existence of cybercafés is not always very helpful, as many seem to be priced for Western tourists rather than people on local incomes.

The case for public access

The case for public access is clear. Private access by itself is not enough to make the internet a benefit in which everyone has a share. The leading countries (Finland and other Nordic countries) provide excellent public access even though their rates of home use are very high, because they see the value of everyone sharing in better information and communication. A detailed look at a country like Britain with high and growing take-up of the internet shows that access is uneven and that it is certain sections of the population that are lagging behind in getting the benefits. Public access is bridging this gap to a small but significant extent. The survey already quoted shows 10% of internet users identified public libraries as their place of access, with something like another 2% getting access in other public institutions. This roughly matches the 11% using internet cafés. The figures show a clear increase during the first six months of 2001 (only 6% used public libraries in January 2001). However, they still show the situation before the round of investment announced in 2001 could have had any effect. It is reasonable to anticipate even higher rates of access in public institutions when the provision of public access is closer to being completely spread across the country. In poorer countries, public access is an obvious priority as a means of preventing the worst kinds of social exclusion operating in relation to internet access. However, provision of public access facilities in any country, rich, poor or just jogging along, is not just a matter of preventing social exclusion. It offers the extra potential of access that is supported by professional guidance. Well-managed public access complements private access rather than just providing a place for people who cannot obtain private access to log on.

Managing public access

Why manage access?

There are a number of very obvious reasons why public access has to be managed access. The first and most obvious is a simple matter of accountability: those who pay (governments and ultimately the taxpayers who support them) will expect that provision be made in an organized fashion with outcomes that can be checked. Secondly, providing public access is not just a simple matter of setting up networked workstations in some kind of centre and switching them on. It is more complicated than that.

Computers and network facilities require technical support and that has to be managed. Above and beyond technical support, however, there is a responsibility to provide personal support and guidance to users so that they can make effective use of what is provided. This is a normal function of libraries and other information institutions, but it is also a very specific need with a medium that is unfamiliar to many people and that can present serious complications. The users of public access facilities are likely to include many who are new users, people from groups with little background in information technology (such as older people, or migrants from less technically advanced countries), or those with very precise information needs of a kind that they are used to bringing to a library or information centre. The case for managed access is clear, but the problem is that managing internet access is different in at least two ways from what is already familiar to information professionals.

- There are decades of experience and miles of shelves of textbooks on managing information resources in print and other more tangible forms (for instance, audio tapes or microforms). Some of this knowledge still applies in the electronic information environment. However, the differences are pretty fundamental. First and foremost, as I have already suggested, access to the internet is essentially access to a complete medium and all its resources. This is entirely different from what any existing form of information institition has been able to offer. The information professions have developed their rules and procedures to manage selections and samples of the total information resource in 'hard' formats such as print on paper, not the total resource itself. When you turn to the internet and look at it as a total resource you find that it is largely unsorted, unassessed and unapproved for quality. This means that, as an information professional, you have to find new approaches to the management of the service.
- The second big difference that calls for management is, as I stressed earlier in this chapter, that the internet is interactive. What is more, libraries and other information institutions are more or less obliged to offer the full range of internet services including interactivity. Attempts to provide internet access without e-mail are basically frustrated by webmail services, such as Hot Mail. In addition, it is difficult to exclude newsgroups because they can be accessed via search engines. This leaves the public access

service managing communication facilities, but with virtually no previous tradition or experience of services that include this. Librarians or archivists certainly do not post people's letters for them, or provide them with telephones. Experience also shows that the attraction of the internet to users is at least as much its ability to receive and send messages of one kind or another as it is the availability of information resources of a more fixed type. Therefore it makes sense to accept that people will use public internet facilities for communication purposes, and in doing so accept that you are working in a new resource management dimension.

Difficulties with public access

It would be easy to make it sound as though internet access is not only different from access to physical resources, but that it is superior in every way. This is not the case. internet access is machine-dependent in a way that makes it enormously vulnerable and frequently unreliable. It is only just becoming portable through wireless systems and essentially, for public access purposes, people have to use it in fixed places and in limited numbers. The numbers of people who can use it are limited by the number of terminals and the terminals are limited by the money and space available for them. Ignoring the question of money for a moment, even quite a small library, information centre or learning centre, can accommodate many more users looking at books at one time than it could using computers, even if all the available space were given over to them. Certainly a very full library results in jostling at the shelves, queues at the catalogues and issue desks, but even then, booking systems are only needed for machine-dependent media like microform or audio-listening facilities. The same is obviously not true of internet access, where booking arrangements and limited periods of use are generally required.

Internet use can also be disruptive in a public space in ways that use of print and other physical media is generally not. Reading is essentially an individual activity, and most people can read without pronouncing what they read out loud. Certainly conversation in libraries can be a serious nuisance: hence the signs asking for silence that have bedevilled the reputation of the library profession. Libraries have also always attracted a proportion of disruptive users. People at the end of their tether sometimes have spectacular breakdowns in libraries, and I can witness that a remarkable accoustic like that of the old Reading Room of the British Museum Library could magnify this to heroic proportions. There are also the exhibitionists, masturbators, peepers and molesters who look at books that fuel their antisocial tendencies. However, this is a problem of limited dimensions because libraries generally choose to stock little, if any, actual pornography, and pornography substitutes such as art books are not particularly helpful or plentiful on the shelves.

In contrast, any kind of computer use can be noisy and otherwise distracting to those nearby. Light, colour, movement and sound are parts of the way they communicate with their user, and all of these can draw the attention of unwilling neighbours in a working space. It is also argued very strongly by some people, as we will see in the next chapter, that the internet, as presently structured, is inherently 'unsafe' and even 'dangerous' because of its content. For instance, there is a great deal of pornography and other material that gives cause for anxiety on the internet. In relation to private users in the seclusion of their own homes this may or may not be a problem that concerns the rest of us. In a public space, while they are making use of facilities provided at public expense, someone accessing certain types of material may well be a genuine problem. Information professionals generally control the content of their collections, deliberately or otherwise, rightly or wrongly, in ways that limit the scope for controversy and do not generally incite antisocial behaviour. The internet, as we have already noted, is not, in itself, controlled or limited in this way.

Requirements for good management

Managing public internet access is not simply a matter of reacting to these difficulties and solving the problem of disruption. Well-managed access ought to be not only less problematic, it should also be much more effective for users. Remember, not all the non-users of the internet are people who cannot afford it. Some are people who are not comfortable coping with the medium unsupported. Good management of public internet access should meet a number of requirements that will provide users with the assurance of a high-quality service. These include:

- providing users with access to good, well-maintained technology
- providing access free of charge, or at a charge set on a cost-recovery basis, in the interests of full social inclusion

- providing access to workstations on a well-organized basis so that time on them is fairly shared between users
- offering guidance for new users and support for those seeking information.

At the same time management needs to take account of a number of difficult and contentious issues, the nature of which will be discussed in the next chapter. They include the following, though not necessarily in order of priority:

- protection of human dignity in relation to the availability of
  — pornography
  — materials inciting racial hate, or hostility on grounds of gender, sexual orientation, religion and other beliefs
- protection of children and young people from exposure to unsuitable or harmful material
- minimizing the disruption of one user by another including
  — disturbance of concentration
  — harassment
- protecting staff from harassment by users
- preventing illegal use of the access facilities, including
  — infringement of intellectual property rights
  — defamation
  — fraud and similar computer crimes
- ensuring security from external intrusion, including
  — privacy infringement
  — spreading viruses
  — other forms of intrusion
- respecting confidentiality and integrity of user data
- ensuring information quality in terms of
  — accuracy
  — authenticity.

This is a formidable list. Some of these are old problems for information professionals, but appearing in new and more difficult forms. Some are completely new consequences of the introduction of internet access facilities. All require close attention if they are to be addressed effectively in an institution that is seeking to provide the best quality of service to the public.

As the next chapter will show, not only are the issues themselves very complex, but the guiding principles for dealing with them are often quite difficult to identify and apply.

References

Bangemann, M. (1994) *Europe and the global information society: recommendations to the European Council*, Luxembourg, European Commission.

Global Internet Liberty Campaign (2000) *Bridging the digital divide: internet access in Central and Eastern Europe*, Washington, Center for Democracy and Technology.

Library and Information Commission (1997) *New library: the people's network*, available at
www.ukoln.ac.uk/services/lic/newlibrary/contents.html

National Statistics (2001) *Internet access*, available at
www.statistics.gov.uk/pdfdir/int0601.pdf

Ormes, S. and Dempsey, L. (1995) *Library and Information Commission Public Library Internet Survey*, available at
http://ukoln.bath.ac.uk/services/papers/ukoln/ormes-1995-01/

People's Network (2001)
www.peoplesnetwork.gov.uk/netbase/country/england.html

2
The internet problem

I concluded the previous chapter with the suggestion that public access to the internet needs to be managed partially, at least, because the internet is a problem. By preference, I would not treat the internet as a problem. To me it is a wonderful means of communication and extra source of information. It has changed my professional life for the better and I am well aware that it has done as much and more for millions of other people. However, we cannot ignore the fact that there is a substantial section of public opinion, and professional opinion too, that regards it as a problem.

This chapter will begin with a discussion of the roots of people's unease about, or fear of, the internet. I will then go on to look at the global struggle for control of the internet. The main body of the chapter deals with the specific anxieties over content, under seven headings:

- Harmful content
- Other dangerous content
- Unreliable content
- Commercialization of content
- Intellectual property problems
- Privacy and secrecy
- Cybercrime.

Then, the main approaches to the internet 'problem' are introduced under three headings:

- Legislation
- Policing
- Filtering.

Fear of the internet

Fear of the internet is based on the apparent lack of control that can be exercised over it. Everyone who communicates over the internet or puts up web pages seems to have almost as much control as anyone else. This has led to outbursts of rhetoric from some people who choose to regard the internet as another world in which the conventions and laws of the old one have no validity. John Perry Barlow, a founder of the Electronic Frontier Foundation, put this freedom from constraints at the centre of his exuberant declaration on behalf of what he called the inhabitants of cyberspace:

> We are creating a world where anyone, anywhere may express his or her beliefs, no matter how singular, without fear of being coerced into silence or conformity. Your legal concepts of property, expression, identity, movement and context do not apply to us.
>
> (Barlow, 1996)

This is rather magnificent, but rather imaginative too. In fact, there is much more control, and potential for increased control, than some of us are completely happy with. Yet, if these kinds of claims are made, it is not surprising that law-abiding information professionals are a little uneasy about what they might be letting in through the wires when they introduce the internet into their respectable institutions. The public and professional fears can be summed up as having two main elements:

- First there are fears about internet content itself, clustering around the presence of pornography and other 'dangerous' material. These content-related fears also include very reasonable concerns about the quality and accuracy of information, the real threat to intellectual property as we know it, the commercialization of information, questions about the privacy of communication over the internet, the danger of surveillance (both official and commercial), and interference (hacking and cybercrime) with business and other transactions.
- Secondly there are fears that little or nothing can be done about content, because internet activity is not limited by national boundaries. This means that situations occur in which offences of many kinds (fraud, publication of obscene material, breaches of official security, for instance) cannot be stopped, nor the alleged perpetrators brought to trial.

This is what we read about in the press and what is talked about on TV and radio. However, I do not believe that the real problem of the internet is to do with these specific fears. There is a another economic and political dimension that lies underneath all this. Powerful players are shaping the future of global communication generally, and the internet in particular. For the information professional the directions in which these forces are moving is not entirely encouraging. It does not fit very comfortably with their not-for-profit ideal of providing information for the public good.

Control of the internet

For convenience the players in this global power game can be divided into three broad groupings.

- First there is an official sector, expressing itself through the international bodies created by treaties between governments: the European Union, the Council of Europe, UNESCO, World Intellectual Property Organisation (WIPO), the Group of Seven Industrialised Nations (G7), the Organisation for Economic Cooperation and Development (OECD), the World Trade Organisation (WTO) and others.
- Secondly there is a commercial sector consisting not only of business corporations from the media and communications sector, but also others in finance, services and retailing that do business on the internet.
- Finally there is a less well-defined sector, that can be called the civil sector. It consists of an enormous variety of non-governmental organizations (NGOs) representing some aspect or other of civil society. It is with this sector that most information professionals tend to identify, even though their institutions are usually within the public or state sector.

World trade and the internet

The official sector and the commercial sector may not always entirely agree over the regulation of business activity on the internet, but alliances between them hold the key to the internet's development. The common theme of the international trade negotiations of the late 1990s was the creation of a trading environment with national barriers to the movement of goods and services more or less totally removed. The internet already offers the free flow of content in practice. When that free flow is backed by a trading environment in which corporations can turn to international regulatory bodies to have surviving barriers removed, there is an open field for what has been described as the commodification of content (Shrybman, 2000). The major media corporations, with their great holdings of intellectual property rights in information and cultural content, will effectively be able to dictate the terms of access to content anywhere in the world. Many representatives of the civil sector fear that the present chaotic but fertile mix of commercial, not-for-profit, and entirely amateur content on the internet will not survive this process.

The civil sector and the internet

A revulsion against the general trend of the global trade environment has led to the disruption of a number of major world negotiating forums, such as the World Trade Organisation (WTO) discussions at Seattle in December 1999. On that occasion civil sector organizations connected with the information world, including the American Library Association and the Canadian Library Association, took observer status at the talks. Their aim was to lobby in favour of the present diverse and open communications environment, as represented by the internet. Information professionals are also involved in the less formal opposition to globalization. One of the protesters arrested and subsequently imprisoned at Gothenburg during anti-globalization demonstrations in 2001 was a library staff member from London. His protest was not exclusively focused on the information dimensions, but it illustrates the strength of concern that does exist within the sector. However, the role of the civil sector in this global manoeuvring is not straightforward because of the variety of viewpoints the sector encompasses.

Within it are out and out libertarians who are strong within organizations such as the Electronic Frontier Foundation (EFF), or the Global Internet Liberty Campaign (GILC). Both of these campaign for a restriction-free internet. EFF has set up a Blue Ribbon campaign, which encourages websites favouring freedom of expression to carry the blue ribbon motif. At the same time, other organizations from the civil sector are very much in favour of controlling the internet. For instance, some feminist groups regard the internet as a medium with content that is used to harass, exploit, control or demean women. They focus very strongly on the need to suppress pornography.

As another example there are the groups that seek to protect children from exposure to pornography and to prevent paedophiles using internet chat facilities to lure children into danger. There is a substantial network of British organizations (the National Society for the Prevention of Cruelty to Children, the Children's Society, the National Council of Voluntary Child Care Organisations, the National Children's Bureau, and others) that are active on the issue of the internet. They co-operate in a Children's Charities Coalition on Internet Safety. The Coalition in turn liaises with the UK Home Office's Task Force on Child Protection on the Internet, which is looking at a range of initiatives in law reform, policing, industry self-regulation, and schemes to help young people use the internet with awareness of the dangers that they may encounter. Much the same group of players is associated with an Online Networked Children's Education project (ONCE) at the University of Central Lancashire, funded under the European Commission Internet Action Plan. This seeks to involve young people and teenagers in formulating and developing online safety guidelines. The organizations are debating the issues, exploring different approaches and co-operating widely.

It would not be unfair to suggest that the best informed and most open debates on internet freedom and control take place within the civil sector. However, the economic power lies with the commercial sector and the ability to regulate with the official sector. Although this chapter is about the issues and the debates, it is always important to remember the global dimension and see the issues in terms of the sources of power and influence.

Harmful content

When people describe internet content as harmful they tend to lump together both legal and illegal material and, although there are other categories, they are most commonly talking about sexual content. The actual legality or not of a particular item of content may well be open to dispute, and this varies very considerably between different jurisdictions. Chapter 4 deals with some of the legal aspects, while this section just deals with people's perception of sexual content as a problem on the internet. This perception is so strong that you could say that it is more or less universal. Therefore it is essential for information professionals to have an idea of the extent to which sexual content is actually available and how far this is significant. As soon as we look into this question, it becomes obvious that this kind of content is very widespread indeed.

Sexual content

Pornography intended to bring profit to those who have placed it on the internet is there in such great quantities that it has arguably been the chief motor for the commercialization of the internet. Figures drawn together from various sources by Cronin and Davenport (2001) suggest that the USA has an estimated 30,000 pornographic websites generating revenue from subscriptions, advertising and merchandizing. As long ago as 1998 the so-called 'adult business' on the internet was estimated to have generated revenue of anywhere from $500 million to $1 billion with increases as great as 30% year on year. Surveys of the terms most frequently used in search engines have consistently revealed sexually related words at the top of the list. The number of visits to sex-related sites is increasing at a great rate: an estimate covering a six-month period during 1999 was that traffic to pornography sites increased by 140%. Although many pornographic sites are small-scale businesses, there also substantial enterprises generating considerable profits. There is also a great deal of sexual content created by users for their own pleasure and that of others in internet communication. Newsgroups that include sexual discussion and the posting of stories and fantasies, in particular alt.sex, have enormous volumes of traffic and a high profile among internet users. A sector as large as this, particularly with the level of business activity it includes, has the ability to stimulate technical developments to support its delivery of content. There is a strong case for saying that the distribution of pornography has influenced the development of technology such as internet chat, online video, multi-server web hosting systems and others.

This large, growing, revenue-generating sexual sector has been the centre of controversy since the mid-1990s, and the nature of this has been well set out by McMurdo (1997). It was statistics contained in a 1994 study of pornography available on the internet by Martin Rimm, of Carnegie Mellon University, that brought internet sex into the centre of public debate. He claimed to have identified over 900,000 images with sexual content available over the internet during a short period. The accuracy of Rimm's figures is less important than their entry into the public mind as benchmarks for the presence of this type of content. Since then sex on the internet has been exhaustively debated in newspapers and magazines, the professional press, radio and TV programmes, on the internet itself, by politicians in and out of parliaments, and in conversations and discussions between individuals and groups of people. Some of the comment simply alleges that it is harmful to society generally, but a great deal of it is specifically focused on potential harm to children. As usual in debates on the effects of sexual images and ideas, the precise way in which this material actually does harm is not explained but taken as given. Despite this gap in the argument, the anxiety is too great to be ignored. Providers of public access to the internet, among all the others involved, need to know just where they stand on the issue of children and internet sexual content.

Accessibility of sexual content

In purely practical terms, it is important to have a sense of how genuinely accessible pornographic content is. First of all, we have to accept that really ingenious users of any age can trace the material they want however difficult the search may be, and can overcome any barriers put in their way to get access to it. But just how likely is it that the unwary, particularly the unwary and underage, will inadvertently access such material? They can certainly come across a certain amount without too much trouble. The masturbatory fantasies posted to newsgroups are certainly easily available, and material posted by amateur pornographers sometimes appears with deceptive titles and URLs. This is either to escape notice, or to lure in the unsuspecting, probably with deliberate intent to shock and offend. When lecturing on this topic recently, I noticed an embarrassed stir among the group. It emerged that only the same day a male member of the student group had suggested that a female member of the group should look at a site bearing the name of a popular female DJ. He was well aware that this was in fact a pornographic site and he had been amused at her reaction to discovering this. The class continued with a fruitful discussion about harassment based on this example.

Commercial pornographic sites are also easy to locate. An important point about most of these, however, is that after viewing some images provided as free 'tasters' it is usually necessary to fill in a registration page to explore the full site. In fact, registration systems and warning pages make the frequently made suggestion that anyone can almost accidentally happen on extreme commercial sexual content (bestial or paedophilic, for instance) look like an exaggeration. Registration usually requires giving details including a credit card number, but there are also sites providing age authentication services for people wishing to register as users of sites that apply an age barrier. The commercial sex sector on the internet certainly claims that these systems prove that they sincerely set out to limit access to consenting adults only. What is true is if you do enter a commercial pornographic site, you will find it extremely difficult to leave. This is not because of the seductiveness of the images, but because the designers have created a kind of virtual maze from which you may despair of finding an exit.

Child sex aspects

The highest levels of anxiety about children and the internet arise from their possible vulnerability to the activities of paedophiles. This has two aspects. First there is child pornography. In the making of this type of material children are abused, and its accessibility may encourage other potential child abusers. Secondly, paedophiles are accused of using chatrooms to 'groom' possible victims, and to lure them into situations in which their safety is put in danger. There is plenty of evidence that both of these dangers are real. The police in various areas of Britain have investigated and obtained convictions against a number of people for their involvement with child pornography on the internet. For instance, in February 2001 seven men were convicted for their participation in a major internet pornography ring, known as the Wonderland club. There is plenty of anecdotal evidence of children lured into unsuitable exchanges of messages or downright dangerous meetings, and in October 2000 a man was sentenced to imprisonment by a British court after he had used a chatroom to entice a 13-year-old girl to his home for sex. For everyone other than a few ultra-extreme libertarians this type of use is way beyond the bounds of acceptability. The problem both in terms of how governments and police services deal with internet content, and how providers of public access administer their facilities, is how they can succeed in outlawing paedophile content and communication without damaging important freedoms for both adults and children.

Other dangerous content

Anxiety over sexual content is not the only concern. There is also other disturbing content that tends to be swept up along with sexual material in discussions of a 'safer' internet. There is material of an obviously dangerous kind such as bomb-making manuals. For instance, *The big book of mischief – the terrorists' handbook*, has been available via the newsgroup rec.pyrotechnics. This is not the only example. Another website, provided by someone using the alias Candyman, is a collection of information on topics such as drugs, phone phreaking (as the use of technical ingenuity to obtain free phone calls is known), techniques for killing people with the bare hands, and bombs. His justification for this is important because it exposes the dilemma that an information professional might have over material of this kind. He claimed that:

> My actions are those of a librarian or archiver of information. The action of authoring, archiving, or publishing information is protected in the United States Constitution under the First Amendment.   (Wallace and Mangan, 1996)

The problems that this defence creates are also there with the websites and Usenet groups that contain what is described as 'hate speech'. Common examples are those that focus on denial of the Holocaust in which millions of Jews and other minorities died during the World War 2 (Capitanchik and Whine, 1996). Other expressions of racism, misogyny, anti-gay, anti-religious and similar abuse can also easily be encountered on the internet. What such abuse might lead to is illustrated by the Nuremberg Files website case. This site attacked the activities of a list of over 200 named doctors known to practise abortion, accusing them of crimes against humanity. The names of some of the doctors who had been murdered were shown struck out. In February 1999, a court in Oregon, USA, ruled that the site was 'a true threat by one or more of the defendants to do bodily harm, assault or kill any of the plaintiffs'. However, in early 2001 this verdict was effectively reversed on appeal, on the grounds that it was an infringement of the First Amendment rights of the defendants to free speech. There is clearly a real moral and legal dilemma over this type of internet content and no easy answers to be found.

Unreliable content

The thoughtful user and the alert information professional quickly become aware that internet content is often less than what it seems. An area of internet content whose reliability is very uneven is the 'professional' guidance that many sites offer. For example, there is a great deal of health information and advice from different complementary medicine perspectives. Some of this material is of perfectly good quality, but some is misleading and downright dangerous. Much of the time, you don't actually know who is advising you. Lewis (2001) cites examples of young people who have used the anonymity of the internet to pose successfully as experts in different fields. In one particularly striking example he tells of a 15-year-old boy who offered his services on a website called AskMe.com. This was a site on which supposed experts responded to the questions of the public. Largely on the basis of things he had picked up from TV programmes he offered legal advice that he had no trace of a qualification to give, and answered the questions of a large number of people. He may have done a great deal of damage during the course of this, though perhaps not as much as if he had offered medical advice.

Of course unqualified advice and inaccurate information are available in any format that you care to use: the internet is not unique in this. Information professionals, however, generally seek to provide information that they can endorse on the basis of their expertise in selecting reliable and accurate sources. If they offer unmediated access to the internet, they are automatically offering access to a certain amount of content that is unreliable to an extent they would never have permitted in their own collections. This is because there are no controls and quality checks of the kind that a library applies to the documents that it acquires and the information that it provides. There is a lack of good provenance for content, and a tendency for some of it to be borrowed, stolen, distorted or misrepresented. The user is therefore open to the dangers of misinformation and mischief. Urban myths are circulated, frauds carried out and practical jokes played.

A certain amount of knowledge of how to interpret what appears on screen helps in distinguishing the bogus from the reliable. A URL might, for instance, contain the name of some respected news organization like the BBC or CNN in the information that precedes the @ sign. At a superficial glance, this might suggest that by clicking on the link, a reliable news source will be accessed. Of course it is what follows the @ sign that really identifies the source, and the information there will show who is truly responsible for the pages. This may well be someone of quite a different description from what the less relevant part of the URL suggests. If you can take the process further and work out from the address just exactly who the responsible persons are, then there may be good indications as to the reliability of the information provided. An incident in mid-1998 illustrates the point. A young man and woman, 'Diane and Mike', supposedly set up the 'Our First Time' website. This offered subscribers the opportunity to witness a videostream of their first sexual experience together: something like reality TV with the sex left in. This seemed on the face of it to be just a new variant of exploiting sex for money. However, more careful examination of the record of the actual providers of the website suggested that this was a fraud on the world's voyeurs by experienced tricksters who had no intention of providing the promised transmission. Not everyone, however, has the skills to make this kind of deduction.

Commercialization of content

The commencement of the permitting of commercial activity on the internet in 1991 led to a significant shift in the nature of internet content. Previous to this, internet material had been either scientific and official on the one hand, or amateur and unverified on the other. The commercial element has changed the balance in subtle ways, but the user is seldom aware of the mechanisms behind it. It is in the interests of companies to try to limit the scope of potential customers' searches and direct them towards their own sites. First of all they want to attract users into their own websites as quickly after the start of a search as possible. This makes search engines crucially important. Commercial organizations provide them, but not as an act of charity. The search engines are generally configured so as to concentrate on a more commercial subset of the internet universe. They also use the data that they acquire about the topics for which a user is searching, so as to present advertisements for supposedly relevant goods and services. After a while this ceases to be something that users notice in the way that they might on first experiencing it.

Once users access a commercial site, it is in the company's interests to hold them there, seduce them with the novelty of what appears on the pages and the promises of the internal links that are offered, so as to increase the likelihood of impulse purchases. In an even less apparent way, the process continues with configuration of commercial sites to hold the user within them for as long as possible. This 'stickiness' places the features that a user will want deep within the site, reached by series of windows and makes it as difficult as possible to find a way out. There are also 'cookies' and spyware that become attached to a user's system. Cookies are small text files intended to help a program identify a site for some reason or other. Only the server that issued them should read them, but other people's cookies can be read by use of a system bug, and this can serve the interests of those who want to target a user with supposedly relevant content. Spyware can be introduced unobtrusively into a user's system along with freeware programs. It downloads banner advertisements, or passes a user profile to an organization that directs advertising at users with 'appropriate' profiles.

The fact that some of this often has laughably crude effects is less important than the way in which commercial calculation tends to pervade a large proportion of internet activity. It does not necessarily offer the user 'bad' information in the sense of inaccurate or out-of-date information. What it does is reduce users' choice and keep them as far as possible in an information environment that will encourage them to buy goods and services. One response to this problem is to install 'firewalls' into the system. These are software devices that protect networked or individual computers from unwanted incursions. However, technical solutions to the problem of commercial manipulation of the internet are unlikely to do more than provide temporary relief from a proportion of the onslaught.

Intellectual property

Intellectual property, broadly defined, is both the main aspect of free content on the internet and the most truly electronic commodity traded on the internet. Certain kinds of trading in intellectual property continue with little obvious trouble, mainly because the trading is a hybrid of virtual and real. The selling of printed books (ordered and paid for online but dispatched by delivery services) by companies like Amazon.com is the chief example of this. The publishing of books on demand, either printed and bound by the supplier or merely downloadable from an electronic database of content, is another. This last type of business brings us into the area of difficulty. Rights holders and their representatives have been saying for years that digitized information is insufficiently protected on the internet. They can indeed point to hosts of infringements and a general climate of hostility among users towards the whole concept of intellectual property, and electronic intellectual property in particular.

Software

Software was for a while the main cause for concern. It has been the practice of some enthusiasts to 'crack' new software products, ostensibly because of the technical challenge this involves. They have then displayed their ingenuity by making these products available to all and sundry via bulletin boards. The software industry sees this as yet another challenge to the security of their intellectual property rights, which are already infringed worldwide to an enormous extent by individuals, organizations and even governments. They have formed organizations like the Federation Against Software Theft (FAST) to identify major centres of infringement and use the law to enforce intellectual property rights. There is a paradox here in that the imaginative software creator does not necessarily see the internet as the kind of threat that calls for a measure of this kind. The Linux operating system is perhaps the best instance of this kind of approach. It was developed by a Finnish student, Linus Torvalds, as a way to offer the community of users an operating system with very high standards, which the community could test and develop according to its own needs and preferences. Its source code is freely available to anyone, though various versions of the system are developed and sold for use in specific circumstances. The whole spirit of Linux is a subversion of the proprietorial attitude of the major software companies, which have aggressively protected their intellectual property rights.

Music and P2P

Also at the top of the agenda of the intellectual property industries is the issue of the unlicensed copying of music using MP3 technology. MP3's file compression facilities offer users the ability to copy music from discs at a quality more or less equal to the original, in personally customized packages. More than this, however, it can also be used with downloaded digital audio content from websites. To the music companies the technology combined with the abundance of music that has been placed on websites offers a terrible threat to their sales of CDs and other recording formats. To some artists, disillusioned with the companies, it offers an alternative way of making a living from their music. Performers as diverse as the Beastie Boys, Chuck D of Public Enemy, Courtney Love and Marillion have been exploring internet-related ways of financing, publicizing, distributing and obtaining revenue from their products.

The picture has been further complicated by peer-to-peer (P2P) technology, in particular Napster, which was launched in 1999. Napster offered users the opportunity to locate and exchange music online with other users whose computers, and digitized music collections, were linked to the internet as servers. Napster held no music itself, but this did not protect it from the music industry, and legal actions have forced it to restructure as a subscription service, paying revenue to the music companies. The P2P movement is not going to go away, however, just because the effects of Napster itself have been blunted. There are loose networks such as Gnutella, with servers devoted not only to the exchange of music, but digitized movies and other content. The ingenuity of internet users interested in obtaining intellectual property without payment seems always to be one step ahead of the rights owners.

The information professional sits somewhere between the two, uncomfortably trying to balance what the law says and what a user-service philosophy suggests. It is essential that when public access is provided that users should be encouraged to respect intellectual property law so that infringements on public machines may be prevented as far as is possible. This has been a great difficulty for academic institutions that provide access for members by allowing them to connect their own computers to the institution's network. At times the P2P traffic has been so intense as to slow down the local network, with annoying effects on users working on tasks that rely on the network's normal capacity. The chief danger for information institutions is that this kind of activity will suck them into exhausting and unprofitable disputes between users and rightsholders.

Privacy and secrecy

Individual privacy and security

Users by and large value very highly the privacy of their communication and internet use, and helping them to protect this is a concern for information professionals. The problem is that the internet is far from being as secure a means of communication as they might wish. There is clear evidence that the data and communication of individuals on extremely important matters are amazingly poorly protected in some cases. Consequently, the fear that financial systems will prove vulnerable to hackers who can then obtain credit card numbers or divert funds in their own direction is a strong one. The banks and companies that trade over the internet assure us that the problem of secure financial transactions over the internet has been solved, but large numbers of people are not at all comfortable. The actual transfers are protected by systems such as Secure Sockets Layer (SSL), but careless administration of sites has led to some very public scandals.

For instance, in July 2000 a customer of Powergen, the UK utility company, went to the company's site to pay his bill online. He accidentally discovered that he was able to get access to full details of thousands of accounts other than his own without any barrier or password security. The data in the files included customers' names, addresses and credit card details. Although the company dealt with the problem immediately, it told the customer that it did not plan to contact the other people whose details had been made insecure in this way. In fact the company disputed the circumstances and claimed that the customer had hacked into their site. When he contacted the UK Data Protection Commissioner (now the Information Commissioner), he was told that it appeared that Powergen had breached the principles of the UK Data Protection Act of 1998, by not providing proper security for the personal data that it held. However, the Data Protection Commission did not plan to issue an enforcement notice in connection with the incident, accepting the company's assurances that there was no longer a problem. The incident reveals the vulnerability to outside access of personal data held by organizations, despite the security systems and procedures that all major companies claim are in place, and despite the legal and regulatory system in force in the UK.

Not surprisingly, some internet users turn to encryption as a means of protecting their communication, but this tends to arouse government concern over security. Strong encryption is obtainable through freely available programs such as Pretty Good Privacy (PGP). The story of this program, and of its American creator, Phil Zimmerman, illustrates the attitude of governments very dramatically. He was arrested and prosecuted by the FBI on the grounds that his program would be available to America's enemies, who might use it for some such purpose as espionage. As an alternative to privately obtained encryption facilities, governments prefer public key encryption. This also offers strong protection, but through programs to which government agencies also hold a key – to be used 'only in emergencies'. The US Congress has debated a Security and Freedom through Encryption measure, known as SAFE. This would impose controls on the manufacture and use of encryption in the USA. No encryption product could be marketed unless it contained a feature that allowed immediate decryption of a user's messages, without the user's knowledge or consent. The British government, both before and after the change of political control in May 1997, has also investigated the licensing of trusted third parties for the provision of encryption services.

Government concerns

Issues of security bring government and its agencies into the internet field in various other ways. For instance, security agencies can show that information is accessed by possible dissidents through all kinds of media. The use of library internet facilities prior to the hijackings of 11 September 2001 and the assaults on the World Trade Center and the Pentagon by some of those involved seems to be well established. In response to the fear of this kind of communication, security agencies already routinely intercept messages on a very large scale. Official (and unofficial) interception can take place while messages are passing through the telecommunications system in much the same way that telephone messages are 'tapped'. The American National Security Agency (NSA), Britain's GCHQ, and the security agencies of some other countries, co-operate in interception activities that they claim are to prevent the use of networks for purposes of terrorism and criminal activities such as drug trafficking and paedophilia. This global system of surveillance, known as Echelon, filters messages for keywords that suggest some sort of illegal activity may be in progress, and then forwards them to the intelligence agencies (Appraisal, 1999). Whatever their views on the necessity for this kind of official action, some information professionals are naturally ill at ease with providing communication facilities subject to general surveillance of this type.

On the other hand, there is the issue of the use of the internet to make public some of the things that governments would prefer to keep secret.

There have been several instances of official secrets being made public over the internet in a way that is much less easy to suppress than with the media previously available. Once posted on the internet, a message tends to be re-posted on newsgroups or websites around the world. The fact that 'mirror sites', based in other countries, reproduce the content of the original site frustrates attempts by the authorities in the original country to suppress a particular item. Richard Tomlinson, a former member of the British secret service agency MI6, exploited the potential of this. He wished to publish a book telling of his experiences with the agency. When the British Official Secrets Act was invoked to prevent him, he threatened to release the text on the internet from an undisclosed server, where it was held in readiness for distribution. Suppression of this form of dissemination would have been virtually impossible, as another example shows. Official attempts were made in Britain to suppress an online journal, *Euskal Herria Journal*, that was said to be a front for ETA, the Basque terrorist organization. Pressure was put on the internet service provider who mounted it, but this was ineffective as the content was still available via a mirror site based in another jurisdiction.

Cybercrime

Activities that could be classified as cybercrime consist mainly of different types of fraud. Computer fraud can merely involve introducing false data into systems, usually with a view to diverting money into the perpetrator's hands, or programming systems to perform some function that has a similar effect. The extent of computer-related fraud is much disputed, but there seems to be agreement that it costs the world's companies millions, and maybe billions, per year. It is also widely agreed that much of it goes unreported by companies unwilling to admit that their security measures have been insufficient to prevent them being victims of fraud. Even the rather vague public awareness of something wrong with system security that this has created is a cause of more generalized anxiety about cybercrime.

Additionally, there is a suspicion that the internet is used for communication in the process of committing other types of crime. Police services allege that the use of encrypted communication for criminal purposes is widespread. The UK National Criminal Intelligence Service (NCIS) claims that hooligans who sometimes disrupt football matches in Britain use internet communication to co-ordinate their activities. The NCIS now regularly searches the internet for password-accessible websites that may be in use for such purposes. There is also the possibility of using the internet for blackmail, extortion and other crimes that depend on access to communication facilities.

Access from a library or other public facility is seen as a way for criminal activity to remain untraceable. This has to some extent entered popular mythology. Mel Gibson's paranoid character in the movie *Conspiracy Theory* describes sending out via a library terminal messages that he does not want traced. Rumours of crimes committed using public terminals circulate, but few information professionals are willing to discuss cases, probably because of the bad light in which this might cast their organizations. What is probably more likely than crime of a 'professional' nature, such as fraud, taking place at public terminals is their use for mischievous types of crime such as hacking into private systems and the speading of viruses. Public terminals could provide a comparatively anonymous source for this type of activity, although the time and seclusion needed would make it unlikely that anyone would do much more than use the facilities for the sending out of ready-prepared material.

Legislation

Legislation seems like the obvious answer to public anxiety about 'harmful' content. The most prominent attempt to use this approach was in the USA. In 1996, the US government passed a Communications Decency Act (CDA) that would have prevented the use of 'an interactive computer service' to 'send' or 'display' any 'patently offensive' material to a person under 18. The history of this measure sums up the divisions that result from attempts to legislate on the issue. On the same day that the CDA was signed into law by President Clinton, a group of organizations led by the American Civil Liberties Union (ACLU), called the Citizens Internet Empowerment Coalition (CIEC), filed a lawsuit that challenged the law's constitutionality. CIEC linked bodies campaigning for internet freedom, book trade bodies, representative bodies from the internet sector, major computer and internet companies and, last but not least, the American Library Association. The grounds for the case were that the law was contrary to the First Amendment to the American constitution, which protects the freedom of speech and publication. Their challenge was successful when in 1997 the Supreme

Court's decision (*Reno v. ACLU*) was that the Act did indeed violate the First Amendment.

Despite this, there is still much legislative activity at both state and federal level in the USA directed towards internet restriction. There have also been moves to legislate for the internet in other countries. For instance, the Australian Broadcasting Services Amendment (Online Services) Act of 1999 was a similar measure to the CDA, but with the emphasis on filtering. It requires the filtering out of sexually, racially and violently offensive internet content, and the restriction of some permitted material to adults only. Other legislation rolls up the control of internet content with creating a general legal capacity to monitor and intercept communication. The South African Interception and Monitoring Bill, introduced in July 2001, is an example of this. It seeks to monitor, intercept and regulate all internet (and postal) communications between South Africa and other countries. All attempts at legislation of these kinds in any country naturally meet opposition from civil sector organizations concerned with protecting freedom of communication. Only in authoritarian regimes such as the People's Republic of China has it proved possible for governments to impose a system of internet regulation, and that has been done mainly in the interests of political control. What's more, the most significant feature of this control has not been the actual legislation under which it is applied, but official willingness to enforce restrictions.

In clear contrast to any of these approaches, the European Union has launched an Action Plan on Promoting Safer Use of the internet, to cover the four calendar years 1999 to 2002. This deliberately avoids legislation and concentrates on three main lines of approach:

- promotion of industry self-regulation and content-monitoring schemes
- encouraging the industry to provide filtering tools and rating systems that allow parents or teachers to select content appropriate for children in their care
- increasing awareness of services among users, in particular parents, teachers and children, so that they can better understand and take advantage of the opportunities of the internet.

Various projects have been set up under the Action Plan, such as INCORE (2000) in which a group of European organizations have been funded to pursue a number of objectives including developing a European rating and filtering system.

Policing

Approaches based on policing alone obviously do not fit within the framework set out by the Action Plan. China and some other Far Eastern countries have achieved a kind of control over internet access through the effectiveness of their policing and security services rather than new legislation and enforcement through courts of law. The decisions of the courts when they are called into play can be shockingly extreme. They include death sentences passed against some Chinese hackers. The policing approach is not, however, exclusive to authoritarian regimes. In Britain, the London Metropolitan Police have consistently used the threat of intensified policing to encourage content and service providers to eliminate pornographic and other 'harmful' content. The dangers of this approach are obvious, for it can require material to be suppressed when neither the legislature or the law courts have ruled on whether specific items of content are illegal or not. Of course legal advice is taken, but this is not the same thing as a test in the open courts. In effect, the internet service providers and British-based content providers are encouraged to police themselves, but to do so in a climate of discreetly imposed pressure.

At the same time Britain also has an internet industry body called the Internet Watch Foundation (2001), which was set up in September 1996. This is, in effect, a response to the self-policing approach. Its original aims were:

- hindering the use of the internet to transmit illegal material, particularly child pornography, and
- encouraging the classification of legal material on the net in order to enable users to customize the nature of their experience of the net to their own requirements.

IWF has worked on rating and filtering, but it also runs a hotline, part-financed under the Action Plan. People are encouraged to use this to report possible illegal material that they discover on the internet. The IWF assesses this material and if it agrees with the opinion that it is illegal, it encourages providers to remove it, and if necessary passes the case on to the police. Much of the time this will act as a barrier between content producers and service providers on the one hand, and the police and the law courts on the other. As such it represents a benign version of the policing approach, compatible with the Action Plan. At the same time, it is possible to view it as a formidable instrument of informal control, capable of dampening completely legal activities in fields such as culture (art with a strong sexual content, for instance) and social welfare (explicit material on sexual orientation or sexual health).

Filtering

Software filtering and blocking of internet content is an attempt to find a neutral solution to the problems of internet access management. It uses the capacities of automated systems to select which content can be accessed and which cannot. Although the term filtering is invariably used as if it meant filtering and blocking to exclude content, it is worth remembering that the term also applies to filtering to select content. Filtering and recommender systems are, in spirit, the same as published consumer reports, which draw together input from people with experience of particular products or services so as to help other potential buyers. An electronic recommender system can help people select internet content by gathering recommendations that users supply, or gather the implicit recommendations in people's use of content (in the form of references to URLs in Usenet postings, personal favourites lists, or the amount of time people spend with a site). The software can take into account factors such as past agreement between recommenders, or combine evaluations and content analysis to produce a recommendation. Used in this way filtering is a helpful process to which no one is likely to object. Various recommender products have been discussed in a special issue of *Communications of the ACM* (Resnick and Varian, 1997).

However, when 'filtering' is used in the public access context, it usually means filtering to block and exclude content. Content can be filtered across a whole network, within a specific organization, at the computer of a family or individual, or by a provider of public access facilities. Software products that can achieve this are easily available and are often referred to by the name of one of the early entrants into the market as 'Net Nannies'. Other products that are, or have been, available are Cyber Patrol, Cyber Sitter, Net Shepherd, Smart Filter, Surf Watch, Websense. In the first place, all of them depend on accurate monitoring of usage. They will keep track of what happens on a network or an indivual computer, recording keystrokes, time and date, name of program executed and the specific workstation on which activities occur.

As an example, SurfControl publicizes its Cyber Patrol software as a secure and customizable means to protect children from websites filled with violence, hate and pornography (SurfControl, 2001). It also points out that it has integrated this into a range of systems and applications such as firewalls, proxy servers (servers that sit between a web browser and an actual server so as to improve control and performance), search engines and ISP services, offering systems protection against security breaches and inappropriate internal usage.

What filtering software does is to identify and block content on the basis of one or more criteria. It can block on the basis of:

- A 'stoplist' of named sites. Someone, usually the software company, has to create and update the list. Users can generally customize the list themselves. The software can also usually be set to exclude all sites except those specifically allowed.
- Particular words, parts of words, and particular types of images (such as those with patches of fleshtone colour). This is also dependent on the creation and management of a list, in this case, of unacceptable words.
- Ratings that have been applied to a site. This can be done by the owners of the site, or by some third-party agency, according to an agreed system. Metadata facilities for a rating to be applied to a site exist, in the form of the Platform for Internet Content Selection (PICS, 2001). PICS will support whatever ratings system is chosen, but the dominant system is that of the Internet Content Ratings Association (ICRA, 2001), an international organization that has taken over the position held by RSACi (Recreational Software Advisory Council – Internet).

Any variant of this is clearly something that individuals are free to apply to their own internet access. Likewise, an organization providing access for a specific purpose, and no other, has the right to apply monitoring and filtering to make sure that purpose is adhered to. It is also arguably an acceptable alternative within a family. Its validity at public internet access points is much more debatable. The attraction of filtering public access is that it avoids the necessity for fresh legislation, and anticipates the possible interest of police or security services, by removing access to contentious material before it even reaches anyone's workstation. But there are good reasons to question whether this is ethical in the context of public access facilities and there are also questions to ask about the effectiveness of filtering in management terms. These two aspects of filtering will be explored in Chapters 3 and 5 respectively.

What information professionals need to do

As an information professional, you are obliged to work within the law, although you may very possibly not agree with some of the legislation that is passed in your own country. If you are a citizen of the European Union you also need to take into account the approaches set out in the Action Plan. At the same time you are an independent individual who is likely to have plenty of expertise on internet matters, and probably a member of professional bodies that will be seeking to develop collective viewpoints and approaches to the issues. You need to be involved in the struggle for the future of the internet so as to ensure a continuing place for public, non-commercial access, free from undue restriction. There are various options open to you, some of them with a higher public profile than others. They include:

- Protecting standards of information quality. Information professionals have developed a whole set of principles of quality assurance for content that they presently apply to print and other materials. As far as possible these need to be extended to internet content.
- Offering the skills of information organization to a wider community. The information professional's highly developed cataloguing, classification and indexing skills are needed so as to develop the metadata that internet content generally lacks.
- Campaigning on information issues. You may not feel that you are the most natural of political activists, but other groups in civil society are always looking for allies in lobbying and campaigning.

But most of all there is a need for information professionals to make sure that they get things as right as possible within their own institutions. The overwhelming need is that you should:

- Develop institutional policies for access. With strong, coherent policies and documentation that articulates them in the clearest possible way, you will not only face difficult situations with more confidence, but will contribute to a better general understanding of how to deal with internet problems.

In the next three chapters I will deal with the legal, ethical and management issues that provide the framework for policy making.

References

Alderman, J. (2001) *Sonic boom: Napster, P2P and the battle for the future of music*, London, Fourth Estate.

Appraisal of the technologies of political control and interception capabilities 2000 (1999) Brussels, European Parliament, Civil Liberties Committee.

Barlow, J. P. (1996) *Declaration of the Independence of Cyberspace*, available at **www.eff.org/publications/John_Perry_Barlow/barlow_0296.declaration**

Capitanchik, D. and Whine, M. (1996) *The governance of cyberspace: racism on the internet*, London, Institute for Jewish Policy Research.

Cronin, B. and Davenport, E. (2001) E-rogenous zones: positioning pornography in the digital economy, *Information Society*, **17** (1), 33–48.

ICRA (2001)
www.rsac.org

INCORE (2000)
www.incore.org

Internet Watch Foundation (2001)
www.iwf.org.uk

Lewis, M. (2001) *The future just happened*, London, Hodder.

McMurdo, G. (1997) Cyberporn and communication decency, *Journal of Information Science*, **23** (1), 81–90.

PICS (2001)
www.w3.org/PICS

Resnick, P. and Varian, H. R. (eds) (1997) Recommender systems, special section of *Communications of the ACM*, **40** (3), 56–89.

Shrybman, S. (2000) Information, commodification and the World Trade Organisation, *IFLA Journal*, **26** (5–6), 354–61.

SurfControl (2001)
www.surfcontrol.com

Wallace, J. and Mangan, M, (1996) *Sex, laws and cyberspace*, New York, Henry Holt and Co.

3
The ethics of internet access management

As a professional providing internet access points for the public, you will be well aware that this involves problems arising from the issues sketched out in the last chapter. The question is how to pick a way through the difficulties and find solutions with which everyone will be comfortable. As part of the answer to this question you need to recognize that what you are dealing with are ethical problems (though they will also be practical problems and may well be legal problems too).

I will begin this chapter with some general words about ethics, including applied and professional ethics. Then I will outline the ethical positions usually adopted in information work, before discussing freedom of information and confidentiality, as the joint planks of current thinking on information ethics. Finally I will tackle the ethics of filtering, as the centre of current ethical debate on public access to the internet.

The domain of ethics

Categorizing problems as ethical may seem just about as useful as it was for Molière's Bourgeois Gentilhomme to discover that he had been speaking prose all his life, but had never realized it. In fact, identifying that the problems are matters of ethics is extremely helpful, maybe even a bit too helpful. Ethics is a branch of philosophy with an enormous literature. Much of the literature is theoretical, but a great deal has also been written on applied ethics. Representatives of many different schools of thought have examined in detail just about every kind of ethical dilemma imaginable. Fortunately it is not the job of this book to act as a guide through the whole realm of ethics, but a few simple pointers are needed. They will not satisfy anyone who has already studied philosophy, or who wants to obtain the profounder insights that are available, but they will help identify the ethical dimension and everyday ways of dealing with it.

Definitions

First of all, how is ethics defined? Although the dictionaries and encyclopedias naturally disagree to some extent over how to express this, most agree that ethics can be described as the branch of philosophy that deals with morality. It involves attempting to identify what is meant by concepts such as 'good', and the development of general theories of morality. The textbooks on ethics identify several main schools of thought, but in practical terms it helps to reduce these to two: the utilitarian and the deontological. A lay person's understanding of the difference between them would be as follows. Utilitarians look forward to the consequences of an action, while deontologists look back to the principles that ought to govern the choices that someone makes.

The utilitarianism of Jeremy Bentham and John Stuart Mill judges actions on the extent that they produce 'happiness' measured by a balance of pleasure against pain, for the individual or the community: 'the greatest happiness of the greatest number'. It does not really judge what is 'good' and it tends to leave out of consideration aspects of the quality of life other than happiness. The deontological approach is most strongly associated with the German philosopher Immanuel Kant. It stresses duties that are defined by sets of values such as those laid down by systems like religions, social customs and observances, or concepts of people's rights. To a certain extent the differences between the approaches are merely a technical matter. Both approaches very often lead to an agreement on what is moral and what is not. The philosophical dispute often tends to be about why something is moral, rather than whether it is moral or not. However, the distinction becomes important on really contentious issues – euthanasia and animal welfare for instance – where the two systems of thought can actually lead to quite different conclusions. Clear thinking on ethical matters is helped by understanding where other people's arguments come from, and what are the sources of our own reactions to these arguments.

For instance, much of the discussion about information issues is expressed in terms of people's rights. In debate, concepts such as the right to communicate and the right to acquire information are often called upon. This is a deontological approach, because it refers back to duties that arise from a particular source: the arguments in favour of universal human rights. Such is the general currency of the concept of rights that it may not occur to most of us that it can be questioned both in principle, and in its application to information issues. A powerful recent critique of information ethics by Wengert (2001) does precisely this. It might seem that if we follow his line of argument and try not to look at what information professionals do in terms of human rights, then we are abandoning the heart of the whole shared enterprise to bring information to the world. This would be to ignore the fact that there are strong utilitarian reasons why society should support the highest levels of public communication and access to information. The utilitarian argument stresses how well-informed people can be expected to behave in an orderly way, be more productive, respect democratic values, tolerate others. People would behave in these ways because with full access to information they would be in a better position to understand how this would make for a society in which they would be safer, more involved in the decisions that were made, and more likely to be treated with respect by others. The earliest public libraries were justified on utilitarian grounds, and modern information services and institutions can be looked at in much the same way.

Applied ethics

The use of ethical principles as a means of understanding the questions that arise in everyday life and making decisions on difficult issues is called applied ethics. There is plenty of useful guidance available on making ethical judgements from first principles and some of this is applied directly to information work. The Markkula Center for Applied Ethics in California, for instance, suggests that a mix of deontological and utilitarian approaches to an issue may be most helpful (Markkula Center, 2001). The following questions can be asked and answers looked at to see if consistent messages emerge that might suggest a line of action:

* Which option would produce the most good and least harm?
* Which option respects the rights and dignity of all stakeholders? Even if not everyone gets all they want, will everyone still be treated fairly?

- Which option would promote the common good and help all participate more fully in the goods we share as a society, as a community, as a company, as a family?
- Which option would enable the deepening or development of those virtues or character traits that we value as individuals, as a profession, as a society?

As well as looking at the possibility of applying principles directly, it is useful also to look at the application of ethical thinking in related areas. An extremely relevant example of applied ethics is the codes of behaviour informally worked out by internet users and referred to as 'netiquette'. These principles were developed to encourage decent behaviour in a little-regulated area. They concern how to deal with insults (flaming), uncontrolled messaging (spams) and the running of internet games, MUDs (defined in various ways including Multi User Domains or Multi User Dungeons, these are internet fantasy games for a number of players), chatrooms, newsgroups and special interest group websites. One codification of netiquette, for instance, is set out in a series of ten points (Shea, 1994). Some ('Forgive other people's mistakes') sound rather trite, but then so, in hindsight, do the beatitudes, which they rather resemble. Others ('Know where you are in cyberspace') only make sense when you know the specific online context to which they apply. Yet their very existence is evidence of an ethical impulse among network users.

Professional ethics

Decision making in professional life is essentially a branch of applied ethics, and is generally referred to as professional ethics. It is professional ethics, rather than ethics as such, that is the subject matter of this chapter. In one sense 'professional ethics' refers to study and debate on ethical issues in professional life. It also means the process of identifying and codifying sets of agreed ethical standards for particular professions. Medical ethics are the most obvious example of professional ethics. They have been both discussed and codified at least since the fourth century BC, when Hippocrates set out the principles that are still referred to as the Hippocratic Oath.

When medical ethics are seen to be flouted, people's sense of outrage is extremely strong. A doctor who fails to take sufficient care that he has the skill to perform a particular procedure, tests unproven treatments on patients without their consent, obtains financial advantage from his privileged position, or sexually exploits or otherwise abuses patients, has obviously disregarded medical ethics. The conviction in 2000 of the British doctor Harold Shipman for murdering 15 of his patients at Hyde in Cheshire, and the later revelation that he was reliably suspected of also killing up to 300 others over a long period of years, made him a double monster as both mass murderer and traitor to medical ethics. However, the issues are seldom as clear cut as this, even though the principles of medical ethics have been developed over centuries and the cases are debated at length in the media and by the whole population. Although ethical dilemmas have a very high profile in medicine, and in some other professions such as law and financial services, they occur everywhere else that there is professional activity. This naturally includes information work of all kinds.

Ethics of information work

The issues in information and library work do not usually tend to be as dramatic as those that occur in the professions that deal with life and death, or the disposal of enormous sums of money. That does not mean that information ethics are unimportant. Information work, like healthcare, education or social work, is a good example of a profession that people enter because of a commitment to what they see as its ethical values. When you became an information professional you probably did not expect to enjoy wealth, power and fame. This loose ethical commitment to information work does, however, need to be translated into a more precise ethical awareness so as to make good choices between policy alternatives. Commercialization of aspects of public information service is a good example of a current issue with a clear ethical dimension. When decisions have been made, it is possible to defend your policies much more effectively if you understand the ethical directions that critics might adopt, and the structure of arguments that will provide a convincing response to their positions. Information work requires ethical approaches and ethical awareness, but the question to ask is whether the information professions have their own distinctive ethic. The answer is that there is indeed a distinctive ethic, developed during the 20th century and still dominant in 21st-century information work. But before explaining it, it helps to know that there were other principles that were more important in earlier days.

The development of information ethics

In the past, libraries, museums, archives and other information institutions were distinctively different from those of today and the professionals working in them followed different principles. If we look back, we find that the first 'modern' types of library, as opposed to the monastic, royal or private libraries of the Middle Ages, generally came into existence in the period from the 17th century onwards. This is also the period in which collectors began to put together 'cabinets of curiosities' containing significant and interesting objects for their own satisfaction and the edification of others. The record keeping of governments, ecclesiastical bodies, rich and powerful families, and major institutions of many kinds, also began to be better organized and more capable of use by antiquarians and historians. However, these evolving information institutions all tended to serve only small groups of scholarly users, and this dictated the principles on which they were run.

These principles could be summed up as an ethical commitment to posterity, an approach that put the protection and care of the cultural artifact (book, record or museum object) first. There is still a kind of folk memory of the almost total dominance of this inward-looking, protective ethos and the silent, rule-bound, unwelcoming institutions that developed and propagated it. Even today the memory of it blights the general image of the information professions. In fact its days as the dominant professional emphasis in librarianship and museum work were numbered once public libraries and museums began to be set up all over the English-speaking world and elsewhere from roughly the mid-19th century onwards. By the middle of the 20th century libraries, museums and archives had all, to some extent or other, adopted an approach with a strong user focus. The spirit of this can be felt in library outreach programmes, the education activities of museums, and the extensive publication programmes of record offices.

In 19th- and early 20th-century librarianship this user focus was particularly important. There was an ethos of social involvement, in which librarians set out to guide the reading of the community, and through this to exercise a positive influence on its thoughts and actions. It was an approach that brought a certain amount of confusion and some distress to librarians, because people did not seem to want to be improved. Librarians felt that their users ought to read improving works when they actually wanted to be entertained by much more frivolous stuff. The 'great fiction debate' that filled so many column inches of the professional press on both sides of the Atlantic at the end of the 19th century showed a profession struggling with the paradoxes of its philosophy. Nevertheless, it was a philosophy that gave a sense of direction to the whole business of library development, collection building and service to users. It naturally went much further in libraries than could ever be possible in museums and archives. Yet the unshakeable commitment of museums and archives to the safety and integrity of their holdings did not prevent them being seen as institutions that could also perform an improving role in society.

In the second half of the 20th century a rather different philosophy of information and library work replaced the dominance of these earlier ones. This was based solidly on the concept of freedom of access to information. Librarians came to feel that it made more sense to respond to what users wanted to know, rather than to tell them what they should know. The logical outcome of this way of looking at things was the belief that no restrictions, or the absolute minimum of restrictions, ought to be applied to what people could find out. World events in the middle of the 20th century helped convince librarians that this meant a full commitment to opposing all forms of censorship. The war against Nazi Germany and the Cold War with Soviet Russia brought censorship issues to the front of people's minds. Then in the USA, the McCarthyite attacks on all things 'unAmerican' actually brought librarians up against attempts to suppress ideas in their own communities. Librarians on both sides of the Atlantic came to see themselves as providing uncensored, 'objective' information, and in Britain this was sometimes described, half in jest, as the creed of the librarian: 'no politics, no religion and no morals' (Foskett, 1962).

Codes of ethics

The current state of information ethics is given succinct and definitive form in codes of professional conduct. Working parties and specialist committees draft such codes, but they get their validity from the fact that their acceptance is endorsed by the membership of an association as a whole. Although they are often backed by a disciplinary procedure, in most cases this is seldom brought into action. Codes work by encouraging good practice rather than enforcing it. What is said in the different codes of library and information associations tends to be fairly consistent, and Hill (1997) sums up the content of codes as: grand principles for the common welfare, which he calls 'Ethics for High Days' and principles that apply to ordinary working practices, or 'Everyday Ethics'. Both categories can be found in the published codes and both are necessary. They provide both a long view of issues and advice that can be applied immediately. It is the long view, the ethics for high days, that I want to consider here.

The most prominent source of guidance is the American Library Association. It has had a clear and unequivocal code since 1938, and this has been revised on more recent occasions (see Appendix 1). The first clause in the code is a statement of commitment to the highest level of service to users. Putting users first implies a concern with all kinds of aspects of the quality of the service that is offered to them, and Clauses 2 and 3 of the ALA Code immediately put this in a context of intellectual freedom, and the user's right to privacy and confidentiality. Indeed, looking at the ethics of the information professions generally suggests that what they have most strongly in common is a concern with quality expressed in terms of:

- freedom of access to information, and
- confidentiality between information professional and client.

These principles can be found in other relevant professional codes, though the emphasis is naturally different. For instance, the ten clauses of the Code of Ethics adopted by the International Council on Archives (see Appendix 1) begin by emphasizing the archivist's duty to archival material, but Clause 6 deals with 'the widest possible access to archival material' and impartial service to all users, and Clause 7 balances respect for access with the privacy of those who are the subject of records. The Code of Professional Responsibility of ARMA International, the Association for Information Management Professionals (see Appendix 1), begins with five social principles. The first deals with supporting the free flow of information and opposition to censorship, the third condemns the unethical concealment of information and the fourth respects the privacy of individuals. Of the eight professional principles that follow, the sixth is in support of the confidentiality of privileged information. Even the very detailed International Council on Museums' Code of Professional Ethics (ICOM Code, 1986), although clearly reflecting the great significance of collection-related matters, also includes these two principles of freedom of information and confidentiality. Clause 2.6 states that the museum is an institution in the service of the whole of society, and 2.7 calls for the maximum public access to collections. Clause 7.3 deals with various aspects of confidentiality in the context of museum work. It is these two principles that I will use to structure the sections on information ethics that follow.

Freedom of information
Origins of the idea

Freedom of information is a simplified way of talking about two ideas that are distinct from each other but which make very little sense if they are separated: freedom of expression, and freedom of access to information. If we only use the term freedom of information, it sounds as though we mean freedom for something that is abstract – information – when actually we are talking about freedoms for people. In the first place we mean their freedom to communicate with others, whether individuals, groups, or just anyone who will listen (freedom of expression), and secondly their freedom to receive communication from others (freedom of access to information).

In the past the emphasis tended to be on freedom of expression. The idea dates back at least to the Greek philosophers of the centuries BC. Today it is recognized in all the major international agreements on human rights, most importantly the UN General Assembly's Universal Declaration on Human Rights, 1945. Article 19 of the Declaration states that:

> Everyone has the right to freedom of opinion and expression; this right includes the freedom to hold opinions without interference and to seek, receive and impart information and ideas through any media and regardless of frontiers.

However, Article 19 goes beyond a simple freedom of expression, to include the rights to 'seek' and 'receive'. These guarantee members of the public the access to the information that they and others have the right to impart. Freedom of access to information is something that citizens want and they prove it by buying books, newspapers and magazines, and making constant use of broadcast and networked media. They expect the media to give them the information that will allow them to form their own opinions on topics of public interest. Seeking and receiving information are also central to the activities of information professionals of all types, and the presence of these principles in the UN Declaration is the strongest possible endorsement of their work.

Implications of freedom of information

Freedom of access implies more than just recognizing an abstract right to access. Without the practical means to obtain access, the right could be more of a source of frustration than an encouragement to believe that all is well for the information seeker. First of all there needs to be freedom from hindrance to access by anyone controlling and censoring media. At the same time the principle points the way towards people's access to information and communication, and its spirit is reflected to some degree or other in the constitutions and laws of many nations. At the same time we know that the majority of the world's governments practise censorship in a wide variety of forms, and that even the most open and democratic governments retain certain powers to limit what can be communicated. For instance, limitations on grounds of national security are more or less universal. Sometimes governments take ethical decisions on behalf of the population, as when they censor on religious or moral grounds. Other common limitations of the principle seek to protect the impartiality of the judicial process by limiting what can be said about current legal cases, and there is prohibition of communication that might threaten public order and good relations between parts of the community (such as the provisions made in the British Race Relations Act).

Despite its incompleteness in practice, freedom of access is an important justification for the provision of public information facilities. It can be argued that the principle implies that everyone should have an equal opportunity to obtain information. If we accept this, it is not good enough that the information is in print somewhere, or is broadcast or available over the internet. If these sources are restricted to those who can pay for them, that is a kind of an infringement of the right to information of those people who cannot afford them. It is to overcome this problem that governments provide shared access through libraries and other public information institutions. In the information-rich democratic countries of Europe and North America this means that any citizen who wants to know something should be able to get it from the library. Yet we all know that even in privileged parts of the world what libraries can acquire is uneven, and what the user wants may not be there. Up until the age of the internet, getting access to materials that the library had to obtain from beyond its immediate holdings was even less straightforward, and even the internet is not a universal answer to the problem.

This is why the information professions have developed a concept of freedom of access to information that concentrates on expanding the practical means for access. In 1982 IFLA, with the support of UNESCO, put forward the principle of Universal Availability of Publications (UAP), and at the IFLA Congress in Chicago in 1985 proposed broadening this into Universal Availability of Information (UAI). The latter is obviously the more powerful concept, but IFLA has concentrated on its UAP programme, which is co-ordinated by the International Office for UAP based at the British Library Document Supply Centre, Boston Spa. Cornish (1998) stresses that 'access to published information is essential for human development in all areas of life', and UAP programme activities concentrate on improving the publication and supply of materials, library acquisitions, and interlending and library co-operation.

By itself this is not enough, because it deals mainly with published information (including by implication material that is 'published' on the internet). Other documentation, most particularly the files held by governments and their agencies, contain enormous quantities of information that people may desperately need. A right of free access to official information is an essential aspect of a complete vision of freedom of access. There is evidence of some expansion of freedom of information in progress, and I will discuss freedom of information laws in the next chapter. However, for our purposes the important thing to remember is that freedom of information may be a key ethical principle for libraries and other information institutions, but the access to information that they are able to give is only a segment of what is called for by a full interpretation of the principle (Sturges, 2001).

Confidentiality

Confidentiality in the library of print

Respect for client confidentiality fits into the practice of information work because it provides a natural complement to freedom of access. If we examine what users of information services are looking for, it is clear that while they want most things to be matters of open communication, they also want things connected with themselves kept private. In the past this has not really been seen as a problem. It was possible for users to take advantage of most public information resources with very little formality. Browsing for information and making enquiries to staff could often be done in complete anonymity. Public displays in museums were open to anyone, and the full holdings of museums and archives could often be accessed just on the basis of a signature in a visitors' book. Library membership was usually available after presenting only basic proof of identity, and members could borrow from collections with little restriction. Because libraries generally used methods like the Browne card system, when readers returned the books that they had borrowed, no record remained of what they had taken.

Information professionals seem to have felt little need to monitor the type of material in which their users were interested, unless it was in order to provide them with greater help. In some libraries the user was required to sign for valuable material and to use it only at a desk that could be supervised, so as to minimize opportunities for razoring out prints, or other nefarious activity. This kind of precaution was the exception rather than the rule in libraries, though it is naturally standard procedure in archives, where all the material is unique. Among themselves, information professionals certainly commented on the material that interested users. Nevertheless, librarians did not actually stand over users of books checking whether what they were looking at presented moral problems, nor did museum curators monitor the time visitors spent looking at statues of nudes or erotic prints. It is true that quite a few libraries kept art books with pictures of nudes, marriage guidance books, sexual health manuals and some controversial novels in a closed store. These were accessible on request with only the barrier of embarrassment to overcome. The public library that I used as a boy employed this method and it certainly inhibited me from asking for quite a lot of material I would have liked to have seen. In general terms, users of most kinds of material were usually given the benefit of any doubt and allowed to consult what they chose, without professionals feeling a need to know what they were doing. In such a climate it was easy to preserve confidentiality.

Confidentiality in the electronic library

More recently, the confidential relationship between user and professional has been placed under strain by the accumulation of user data in electronic systems. In principle, information professionals should no more stand over users of the digital library and control what they consult than they did with the users of books. In practice, there are both pressures and incentives to do just that. The pressures consist of the need to respond to public fears that cluster round pornography on the internet and the danger it is felt to present to children and others. There is also a need to take into account the genuine interest that police and security services have in the communication and information use of people they suspect of committing or planning criminal activities. The records exist and, as an information professional, you may need to decide how far they are protected by the principle of confidentiality.

The incentives are the possible benefits to the service of exploiting electronic files of user data. Estabrook (1996) argues persuasively for institutions to do precisely that. She suggests that users might appreciate being alerted to the availability of resources that match their interests on the basis of personal profiles built up from data about their previous transactions. However, once profiles of this type have been collected and organized, there is also potential for their sale or licensing to commercial organizations. Again this might be something that users would find acceptable, and the appearance of advertisements for online booksellers like Amazon.com on the home pages of library OPACs does not seem to have brought protests. But, taken a step or two further it could result in obtrusive marketing, not just of books, but other products supposedly appropriate to a user's interests.

A study that I directed in Loughborough University's Department of Information Science (funded by Re:source, the UK Council for Museums, Archives and Libraries) threw light on the current state of the confidential relationship (Sturges, Teng and Iliffe, 2001). During 2000 and 2001 project staff investigated the issue from the perspectives of both users and information professionals. Results obtained by the time of writing this book suggest that users are wary of commercial intrusion, but that they trust information professionals to protect the confidentiality of the data the institution holds about them. This is rather reassuring on the face of it. The problem is that information institutions are shown by the research not to be particularly well organized to protect the data.

Information ethics in practice

The Loughborough research suggests that all is not necessarily well with the preparedness of information professionals on confidentiality issues. Before going on to discuss what is probably the key issue of information ethics today

– filtering – it is worth looking at some disturbing implications of unquestioning reliance on the joint principles of freedom of information and client confidentiality. Two investigations of library reference services show up the difficulties very well. Both used unobtrusive testing. Unobtrusive testing is a method that is ethically interesting because it uses people (in this case, librarians) as research subjects without previously obtaining their consent. In a chapter that is about the importance of ethical approaches to information and library work it is necessary to apologize for using research that does not fully conform to research ethics. The examples are compelling, however, for what they suggest about the ethical approaches that librarians actually demonstrate when responding to the demands of users.

In a particularly revealing study by Hauptman (1976), librarians' responses to a request for information on an ethically sensitive topic were unobtrusively tested. Hauptman asked at library reference desks for information on explosives, while conveying the impression that his motives for the enquiry might be dangerous. He met with instant compliance on every occasion the test was made. The librarians seemed not to be thinking about the ethical implications of their actions, except insofar as it was part of a confidential transaction with a member of the public that resulted in the user getting the access that had been requested. Interestingly, although some professional debate did follow the publication of this research, it was fairly low key and was not brought to any resolution.

More recent experimentation in quite another social context suggests that the same seemingly passive acceptance of the freedom/privacy principle remains intact. Slovenian researchers tested the acceptance of the national library association's newly drafted code of ethics in their small, newly independent, formerly socialist, Catholic country (Juznic et al, 2001). They found, among other things, that Slovenian librarians unquestioningly handed over helpful material to a researcher purporting to be contemplating suicide. This might, or might not, have been an appropriate response, but it is the implication of moral passivity that gives cause for concern. Codes of ethics are not intended to take ethical issues out of the arena of debate, but to provide practitioners with guidance on decision making. This is the substance of the critique of current information ethics developed by Wengert (2001). This line of argument does not, however, undermine the value of the principles of freedom of information and client confidentiality in themselves. Used as the basis for positive approaches to information problems they are still highly effective, and they lie behind my examination of the ethics of filtering internet content in the next section.

The ethics of filtering

In Chapter 2 I set out some of the reasons why internet access has aroused high levels of concern and also outlined the functioning of filtering, which is generally the most popular solution to this problem. The use of filtering software to block access to internet content is often talked of as if it were merely a technical matter, but in fact it is almost entirely a question of ethics. First of all, people worry about access to internet content in their own homes. When they are simply worrying about their own individual access, it is a matter of personal taste and personal ethical standards. The immediate answer to their problem is at their own fingertips. They can avoid accessing material that they might find distasteful and put its possible existence out of their mind. If they accidentally access offensive material they can hit the BACK button and surf in a different direction. It is true that someone might find even a brief glimpse of some material deeply disturbing, but even then they are not compelled to explore it any further. If they do, they must take responsibility for this, and for putting themselves in a position to find whatever it is. Their response might be that they wish to forget the experience and try to avoid it ever happening again. Their method of achieving this might well be to acquire filtering software, or activate a filtering system already loaded on their computer.

Filtering in the workplace

Very often the worry goes beyond an individual's own wish to preserve their everyday equilibrium from disturbing intrusions. They might well decide that the issue is broader and that they also have some kind of public responsibility, for instance in the work or office context. Pornographic images and text from the internet are sometimes blatantly displayed or circulated in office e-mail systems with a clear intention of giving offence to colleagues (particularly women colleagues). Managers have an obvious responsibility to prevent this, so that employees can carry out their duties without gratuitous interference. Disciplinary measures, including dismissal in one or two high-profile cases, have therefore been taken against employees who have initiated this kind of thing. Rather more difficult ethically are cases involving downloaded files of pornographic material left on the hard disks of computers used by an employee, that might also be used by colleagues. Such cases have also attracted disciplinary measures, on the grounds that an unsuspecting discoverer has been harassed. It could well be claimed that in such cases the person responsible for the computer had not harassed anyone, but had suffered an invasion of privacy. Their real offence was personal use of company facilities. Monitoring and filtering the company's system are obviously attractive forms of intervention. They seem capable of preventing the occurrence of this kind of delicate managerial problem, and allow management to argue that reasonable care has been taken.

Filtering and children

Most often, however, people worry about internet content on behalf of children, and more particularly, their own children. Many parents are afraid of the bad effects that might come from their children reading text that contains dangerous ideas, and looking at graphics and video that contain obscene images. They are also afraid that they might begin exchanging messages with potential corrupters. To a great extent the answers are in their own hands. If children access the internet from home, parents have the responsibility to discuss their internet use with them and also have the ability to restrict their use. Filtering systems are frequently advertised as permitting parents to control their childrens' internet use.

Yet it is not straightforward for a parent to decide just how to handle this, despite the general presumption that parents will prefer to filter. Some parents are actually wary of imposing their own views on their children and would consquently be uneasy about using filtering. For the anxious parent there is actually plenty of guidance on how to help their children use the internet safely. For instance, the UK Department for Education and Skills has a set of guidelines, prepared by Childnet International, on safe use of chatrooms. These advise parents to check, among other things, whether chatrooms are moderated, have proper access control and password verification, and clear sets of terms and conditions of use. Examples of sets of rules for safe internet use that parents can teach to their children, can be found in various places on the web (see Appendix 2). What these guidelines concentrate on is communication between children and their parents about what sites they use, and what happens while they are using them. They also stress that children should not give away address and password details, or make appointments to meet people in the flesh without permission.

The complications are even greater when children use a public institution for their internet access and parents no longer have that degree of control that many consider their right. If a child's internet access is via school facilities, parents generally expect the school authorities to act *in loco parentis*, and this generally means restricting access by some method, most usually filtering. In a way this is not hard for a school to swallow, even though the views of parents on what is acceptable and what is not will vary considerably. Schools do have a set of well-defined objectives connected with student learning, and in the past they have provided hard-copy resources almost exclusively intended to support these objectives. Filtering can be seen as merely ensuring that access to resources is appropriately focused on the learning objectives that have been decided.

Children's rights

In relation to both the family and the school it is usual to talk as if the ethics of the matter were not open to dispute. This does, however, avoid the issue of the autonomy of young people and the question of when they obtain a right to choose what they access. Some parents might accept that their children should make unhindered choices from a very early age, others would wish to retain their control until their children reach the age of legal responsibility. Many teachers might well feel that the ethics of the education professional commit them to encouraging independent thought and information use from as early an age as possible. They might question whether schools, or even parents, actually have a right to restrict the information access of the young people in their care.

In questioning this they are not without powerful support. There is a whole body of international law and statements of principle on children's rights (see Koren, 1996) which rather tends to be forgotten in the debate on filtering children's internet access. The United Nations Convention on the Rights of the Child (United Nations, 1989) is undoubtedly the key document. Its provisions apply to young people up to the age of 18 and set out in detail how the law should both protect and respect their rights. In particular, Article 13 affirms that the right to freedom of expression (including the rights to seek and receive information) applies to children as well as adults. Article 17 specifies that states should ensure that children have access to information and material from a diverse range of sources and media, including books published for children. This Article then goes on to call for 'appropriate guidelines for the protection of the child from information and material injurious to his or her well-being'.

The Convention does not specify the content of such guidelines, but the implication is clear: the child has rights both to information and protection, and the latter should be ensured by means that fall short of an absolute prohibition of access. This is broadly the spirit in which many pressure groups and other interested bodies operate. A body like the UK Children's Charities Coalition on Internet Safety clearly recognizes that filtering will play a part in the precautions that families, schools and other institutions will take to protect children. However, much of its effort, and that of member organizations, goes into guidelines projects aimed at parents, teachers, youth workers and young people themselves. The Children's Society, for instance, was working during 2001 on a set of guidelines for young people involved in the society's projects. These included health and safety advice for computer users, but also guidance on oversight of computer use, education of young people in how to deal with disturbing and unsuitable material in websites and chatrooms, and establishing codes of conduct.

Filtering in libraries

This approach is arguably even more important when we look at public internet access by both children and adults in institutions such as libraries. As we have already seen, the dominant ethos in terms of codes of professional conduct, and day-to-day practice, is freedom of information. Because of the particularly controversial nature of much internet content this is being challenged by members of the public, politicians and, indeed, significant numbers of information professionals. The basic technical case and rationale for filtering was well put by Paul Resnick, then Chair of the working group that developed PICS (Resnick and Miller, 1996). Many information professionals then, and now, rejected that in favour of offering users the maximum freedom of access. This is very much the line argued by the American Library Association and it informs much of the editorial material, comment and reporting of relevant news stories in *American Libraries*. There is, however, a great deal of pressure for filtering from societies in the USA (Family Friendly Libraries, Library Watch, Enough is Enough, Coalition for the Protection of Children and Families, etc.) that exist almost entirely to promote filtering. A cogent case for filtering in information institutions was put by Burt (1997).

What the pro-filtering lobby says is that there is material that they believe is harmful, and some of which is illegal in most jurisdictions, available on the internet. They argue that various measures, including legal action, should be taken against the sources of the material. These measures should include filtering access so as to prevent it being accidentally, or deliberately, looked at by both children and adults in public institutions. As one British librarian put it to me, 'I don't see why my library should be providing pornography paid for from local taxes.' This is very hard to argue against, but it focuses entirely on the negative side of internet content. Experience shows that filtering makes virtually no distinction between what is legal and what is not, and it disadvantages users of legal material, particularly those too diffident to insist on their entitlements. The difficulties are illustrated by cases such as that of Glasgow City Libraries. The library service had installed a filtering product for its public internet access terminals but stopped using it for this very reason. However, in the spring of 2001 a mother complained that her daughter had seen pornographic images at a terminal in the Castlemilk branch. On visiting the library, she found a group of young people around a computer looking at this type of material together. As a consequence of her complaints, Glasgow temporarily discontinued public internet access services until new and (they hoped) more effective filtering had been installed.

The incident encapsulates the whole ethical dilemma over freedom or restriction and the difficulties presented by filtering as any kind of way out of the dilemma. Even the defenders of maximum freedom can often feel beleaguered, and even tainted by the material that they neither wish to promote nor actively to suppress. At the same time those who only wish to extend some protection to children, or to restrict general access to certain extreme aspects of content, find themselves embarrassed by the ineffectiveness of filtering. As an information professional, you may have to decide whether you prefer to protect full freedom of access, or whether you want to filter. This should involve an exploration of the ethical dimensions of the issue, and you will need to take account of the guidance that is available (both from professional associations and from other relevant organizations). Much of this guidance is polarized in one direction or the other, but, in the end, compromise is often necessary. What is quite indispensable is a clear idea of the legal parameters, over which less compromise is possible. It is the law that the next chapter discusses.

References

Burt, D. (1997) In defense of filtering, *American Libraries*, **28** (7), 46–8.

Cornish, G. (1998) Universal availability of publications and its importance to human development, regeneration and growth, *Library Management*, **19** (8), 480–5.

Estabrook, L. (1996) Sacred trust or competitive opportunity: using patron records, *Library Journal*, **121** (2), 48–9.

Foskett, D. (1962) *The creed of the librarian – no politics, no religion, no morals*, London, Library Association.

Hauptman, R. (1976) Professionalism or culpability? An experiment in ethics, *Wilson Library Bulletin*, **50** (8), 626–7.

Hill, M. (1997) Facing up to dilemmas: conflicting ethics and the modern information professional, *FID News Bulletin*, **47** (4), 107–17.

ICOM Code of Professional Ethics (1986) available at **www.icom.org/ethics.html**

Juznic, P. et al. (2001) Excuse me, how do I commit suicide? Access to ethically debatable items of information in public libraries, *Library Management*, **22** (2), 75–9.

Koren, M. (1996) *Tell me! The right of the child to information*, The Hague, NBLC.

Markkula Center for Applied Ethics (2001) *Framework for ethical decision making*, available at **www.scu.edu/SCU/Centers/Ethics/practicing/decision/framework.shtml**

Resnick, P. and Miller, J. (1996) PICS: Internet access controls without censorship, *Communications of the ACM*, **39** (10), 87–93.

Shea, V. (1994) *Netiquette*, San Francisco, Albion Books.

Sturges, P. (2001) The library and freedom of information: agent or icon? *Alexandria*, **13** (1), 3–16.

Sturges, P., Teng, V. and Iliffe, U. (2001) User privacy in the digital library environment: a matter of concern for information professionals, *Library*

Management, **22** (8/9), 364–70.

United Nations (1989) *Convention on the Rights of the Child* (General Assembly Resolution 44/25), New York, United Nations.

Wengert, R. (2001) Some ethical aspects of being an information professional, *Library Trends*, **49** (3), 486–509.

4
The law and the internet

The intention in this chapter is to provide a basic outline of relevant law.

It begins with some general points about the role of the law in information work and then discusses legal responsibility, or liability, for the various activities involved in providing internet access facilities. I then ask the question 'What law applies to providing public access to the internet?' and go on to discuss relevant law under two broad headings. These are user-related law and content-related law.

In relation to users I begin by looking at human rights law and explore how this affects the provision of internet access. I then look at other areas of law under which an institution or an individual professional might be held to be in some way responsible for what happens when people are given internet access facilities. This is covered under three headings:

- Freedom of information
- Privacy
- Harassment.

Then in relation to content, I will deal with:

- Obscenity
- Defamation
- Intellectual property.

Law and the information professional

There are two obvious reasons why you, as a provider of public access, need to have a good awareness of the law.

- First, you need to avoid breaches of the law that could lead to you and your organization being sued or brought into the courts for a criminal offence.
- The other side of this is that you need to know the law so as to avoid the kind of excessive caution that would prevent you doing things that it would be both useful and completely legal for you to do.

This is not at all straightforward. Law in any country is generally complex and often framed in language that is hard for an untrained person to understand. This is certainly true of the countries, particularly Britain and the USA, with a common law system that is based on centuries of tradition and relies heavily on past decisions taken in the courts to clarify and supplement the statutes. For this reason it is very unwise for someone who is not a lawyer to advise other people on the specifics of the law, and you would be very foolish to rely solely on any interpretation of points of law by a non-lawyer. Some people would add that you cannot even rely all that much on lawyers' interpretations of the law, but that is a jaundiced viewpoint and probably based on some unfortunate experience or other. None of this means that the public in general, and professionals in particular, should not form opinions of the law. They very definitely should.

Writing as a non-lawyer myself, I can only outline what is relevant law and give an (informed) lay person's view of it. My reason for writing about the law is not so that you can use this book as a legal text. Do not try to do that: there are plenty of legal texts on the shelves that you can use if you have to. And the book should not be used as a source of guidance when you are faced with a specific case that might involve the law: you need to consider consulting your legal advisers if such a case comes up. However, I do want to help you, as an information professional, to develop a view of the law relating to internet access. That will be vitally important in developing policies for use in your own institution. It will also help you to put strong arguments to lawyers if you have to, and to lobby effectively for new laws or amendments to old laws that will reflect the world of information more accurately.

In this chapter I will discuss the relevant law mainly from the example of one country. A truly international survey is just impractical in a chapter of this kind. Since I am British and this book is published in Britain, it is British law I will use. As justification for what is basically a decision that was unavoidable for me, British law is actually not a bad choice. It simultaneously shares the common law tradition with the USA and a number of British Commonwealth countries, while receiving new law from the European Union, where other members have very different legal traditions derived from the Napoleonic Code. British law may seem quirky and complicated, but it does open up discussion of most possible legal approaches to any given problem. Because the country has IT activity of many different kinds (creation of intellectual property, hardware manufacturing or assembly, telecommunications, e-business) at high levels, it presents plenty of interesting cases and examples. Before providing a survey of broadly relevant law, however, it is necessary to discuss whether or not providers of public access facilities are considered by the law to be responsible for what takes place at the computers that they provide.

Liability of a public access provider

British law

In British law legal responsibility is referred to as liability. This is of two kinds, civil and criminal. There is clearly a possibility of a provider of public access facilities being held liable for some form of wrongdoing under either of these.

In lay person's language, civil liability concerns responsibility for matters usually covered by contractual agreements or by a much more general requirement (the law of tort) not to do harm to others, referred to as the duty of care. In cases of civil liability the person who believes that they have suffered harm has to bring a case against the person they believe is responsible for that harm, that is, to sue them in the courts. If the action is successful, the court can order that the offending actions should be stopped (an 'injunction') and can award damages as compensation to the person harmed.

Criminal liability concerns a whole series of offences that the law identifies as being of such significance, or general effect, that the state (referred to as 'the Crown' in Britain) takes up the case, prosecutes in the courts and punishes the offender by means such as fines and imprisonment. Criminal offences include not only extremes such as murder and treason, but many offences that look more technical and, like computer misuse or video piracy, cause mainly financial damage.

Many matters can be the subject of both civil and criminal liability and an offender could find themselves both needing to pay damages and to accept the punishment that the court metes out.

The risk of liability

This is the general position, but I referred to there being a possibility of both civil and criminal liability for the provider of public access facilities. Just how strong is this possibility? A view from the USA (a much more litigious country than most) puts it in proportion.

> Any library that provides Internet access to third parties or employees, or uses a website for disseminating information, has a potential exposure to civil or criminal litigation. The most significant risk is posed by the legal expense to defend the litigation.
> (Nelson, 2001)

This is important. The risk of being involved in a legal dispute exists but, even in the USA, it would be unlikely to come to an adverse conclusion for a library or other information institution. The main problem is the incidental damage (fees and expenses, staff time, staff distress and disturbance, loss of public reputation and confidence, etc.) that would almost certainly be involved. This is a strong enough reason for being organized to avoid even the outside possibility of involvement. This means that managers must act as if there were a real and immediate risk and have policies and procedures that are, as far as possible, beyond serious legal challenge.

First of all it is necessary to make sure that all the contracts taken on by the organization are sound and properly respected. Unless it can be proved that a contract was in some way unfair, it is obvious that there is full responsibility for all the licensing, purchasing and other agreements that have been undertaken. However, civil liability for non-contractual matters (torts like nuisance, breach of confidence and negligence) is not always so obvious. There is certainly liability for the consequences of direct actions by members of the organization that might result in harm to someone. This could apply to the neglect of precautions to protect anyone who might suffer harm in matters, like public use of internet facilities, over which the institution or individual has control. There may be a possibility that this also extends to responsibility for the harm that a user of public access facilities might do either by not exercising appropriate care, or deliberately undertaking something malicious. This is likely to be dependent on the extent to which the institution has made the user's responsibilities clear to them and taken appropriate precautions to prevent them doing harm.

Liability for internet content and users

Users are, however, not the only concern. By providing internet access the institution also associates itself, to some extent, with the content that others provide on the internet. Criminal (and civil) liability for internet content seems to lie clearly with the content providers. Internet service providers, unless they take some sort of editorial responsibility for content, are not responsible in law for that content. This has not stopped various attempts to associate internet service providers with actions against content providers whose material their services have carried. For instance, in May 2000 a lawsuit was begun in the US District Court in Boston against both the website Nambla.org (operated by the North American Man/Boy Love Association) and the internet service provider Verio, on the grounds that the site incited a man called Charles Jaynes to murder a ten-year-old boy. Jaynes's use of this website took place at the Boston Public Library, but there was no attempt to include the library in the case. The case against both the website's operators and the internet service providers was believed unlikely to be strong enough to stand up in court, but the line of argument connecting site, provider and library is a disturbing one.

The strict interpretation of the liability of the provider of public access facilities is, however, not quite the end of the matter. Precisely because the very nature of the internet itself makes it extremely difficult for the authorities to exercise effective legal control of content itself, there is a tendency for them to turn their attention towards ways to control access to material instead. Obvious ways to achieve something of this kind would include controls on public access facilities. For instance, legislators have come up with various measures in the USA that attempt to make federal funding to institutions conditional on the use of filtering systems. Furthermore, the abortive US Communications Decency Act of 1996 attempted to extend criminal liability to those permitting access to certain categories of internet content. This did not extend as far as libraries and other providers of public access facilities, but subsequent legislative attempts have moved that step further. The US Children's Internet Protection Act, passed in 2000, required schools and libraries to install 'technology protection measures' to prevent children from accessing unsuitable content. This measure is being challenged by the same kind of civil society coalition that defeated the Communications Decency Act, but the tendency of American legislation is to move part at least of the responsibility on to the public access provider.

Institutions do already have liability for criminal offences committed by the institution itself and/or the individual member responsible for the offence. There is also a question of whether the provider of public access facilities has any responsibility for criminal acts committed by users of the facilities. The answer here is clearly similar to the one about civil liability. If trouble has been taken to make sure that users know their responsibilities when using the facilities and reasonable precautions are in place to make sure that the system does not actually offer them ready-made possibilities to commit offences, then the institution ought not to be considered liable for what criminals do. This may sound straightforward to you, but it does not to me. Making sure that the institution really keeps its position safe and secure is not something to be complacent about. As I suggested earlier, a knowledge of the law that might apply to public access provision is indispensable, even if only to confirm that there is no obvious problem with any particular area of law. The difficulty with this is to be sure what areas of law actually apply.

What law applies?

Are there laws governing the internet?

Some people have actually claimed that there is no law that governs the internet, because it is essentially transnational. The extreme libertarian view that is sometimes expressed talks of the internet as a new world in which the laws of nations do not apply. The transnational character of the internet certainly makes it very difficult to bring within the rule of law. The people who use the internet, the servers that hold information, the infrastructure through which information is passed, and the transactions that are carried on through the internet are scattered throughout the world. Any one activity that could be considered illegal might involve people, hardware, systems and outcomes that are spread across just about all the possible jurisdictions that the world can offer. Activity that is suppressed in one country, by closing down a particular server, for instance, is likely to start up again immediately using a service in a country with different laws.

It is also true that the internet is not even subject to a single international treaty or regulatory authority. This is despite the great numbers of treaties and other international agreements that have some application to the internet, such as the intellectual property agreements for which the World Intellectual Property Organization (WIPO) is responsible. True, there is the

Internet Corporation for Names and Numbers (ICANN), which manages domain names on the internet. It was set up in 1998 to take over from Network Solutions Inc. (NSI), which had managed this on behalf of the US National Science Foundation. Placing responsibility in the hands of an independent, self-regulatory body with international participation like ICANN may seem to have created a suitable body to exercise more general governance over the internet. However, in practice ICANN has been criticized as secretive and undemocratic, and its moves towards a broader role in internet governance have been resisted. So, people who say there is no law governing the internet are partially right in that there is no effective international regulation.

Whose laws apply?

Just because there is no international body legislating for, and policing, the internet, does not mean that there is no law that applies to the internet. A British lawyer expresses it like this:

> The suggestion that the Internet has no law is born of wishful thinking more than of cogitation. Local laws of each jurisdiction do apply to activities conducted using the Internet. While enforcing such laws presents new challenges, the pan-political nature of the Internet may in fact render it vulnerable rather than immune to the laws of jurisdictions around the world.   (Smith, 1996)

Anybody who commits an offence will have been under the jurisdiction of one country or another at the time. Whether the offence was committed where the accused happened to be at the time, or a networked computer made it possible to commit the offence in some other completely different place under another set of laws, there would still be laws that applied. Likewise, if the person was in one jurisdiction, the server in another and the results of the offence (a fraud, for instance) in a third, the laws of some or all of the countries would apply. There might be great difficulty in first choosing the law of which country to invoke and then actually bringing someone to court in the chosen jurisdiction. There would also be enormous scope for drawn-out preliminaries, possibly including establishing whether someone can be extradited from one jurisdiction to another on the type of charge that has been brought. Nevertheless the possibilities do exist.

The extreme difficulty that the courts in one country have in trying to take effective action against internet-related offences can be illustrated by a French case in November 2000. A French court attempted to prevent Yahoo! from allowing French users to access sites conducting auctions of Nazi memorabilia. These were already excluded from Yahoo's French portal because French law does not permit the exhibition or sale of items with racist associations. What the court was trying to do was to make this effective by preventing access within France to sites that originated elsewhere, but could, of course, be accessed by French users. This required that, in effect, there should be international censorship of content so as to respect French law. This naturally aroused considerable protest and Yahoo! defended its position with vigour. The moral for internet content providers and users is to use great care in trying to ensure that they comply with the laws of the country in which they are situated, and also the laws of countries with which they have important dealings.

Which laws apply?

The question of which specific law should apply is also a difficult one. Most of the statutes that might be relevant in a particular country will very probably have been drawn up and passed in the pre-internet age. Theft is still theft however the property was taken, and murder is still murder whatever the weapon used, but it may not be simple to establish this in the IT context. During the 1980s various computer-related cases in Britain brought under the Theft Act and the Criminal Damage Act failed, and, in particular, two journalists, Gold and Schifreen, made a successful appeal against their conviction under the Forgery and Counterfeiting Act of 1981. They had hacked into mailboxes in the PRESTEL system, but the difficulty in prosecuting computer offences is shown by the very fact that they were charged with forgery. Gold and Schifreen were charged with 'uttering a false instrument', in fact a misappropriated password. The final verdict was that that this constituted something so transient that it did not meet the law's definition of a forged document.

As a direct consequence of this case, the British parliament attempted to solve both the problem of whose law and which law with a new law. The 1990 Computer Misuse Act contains an attempt to cut through some of the geographical complication by claiming jurisdiction over alleged offenders, whether they themselves, the computer or the resulting offence were actually in Britain. Although this might simplify the process of getting a charge set out in any given case, it would still not guarantee that the case could be brought to court if the accused was in another jurisdiction and could not be brought into Britain to answer the charge. To address the problem of what charges to bring, the Computer Misuse Act identified three new offences: unauthorized access to computer programs and data; unauthorized access with intent to commit further offences; unauthorized modification of computer programs and data. The penalties provided were high (large fines and possible prison sentences of up to five years), which shows the importance that the legislators placed on this. However, a fairly small number of successful prosecutions have been brought under the Act. Indeed there is a suspicion that quite a lot of new law might actually be required in most countries if computer and communications offences were to be specified accurately. Be that as it may, any country with a highly developed legal system is already likely to have a number of laws that are relevant to some degree or other to public internet access. The following sections deal with various relevant areas of law.

Human rights law

Fundamental human rights are not only an important concept in ethics, but they have been reflected in the democratic constitutions of states ever since the newly independent USA adopted its constitution in 1789. The most significant thing about the American constitution in relation to information work is the First Amendment, passed along with nine other amendments in 1791 as part of the Bill of Rights. The First Amendment prohibits Congress from 'abridging the freedom of speech, or of the press'. This is interpreted broadly as protecting freedom of expression from almost any kind of interference by the state, but it also serves as a beacon for freedom in all discussion of information and communication in the USA. It is constantly cited when possible threats to freedom of expression are identified, and it has proved an effective test of whether new laws and regulations or the decisions of the courts are compatible with the human right to express opinion, however extreme that opinion might be.

Human Rights Act 1998

Britain is rare in not having a formal constitution and this has meant that certain things that are generally recognized as human rights, and privacy is a very good example, have not been adequately dealt with by its laws. This situation was changed more or less completely when the European Convention on Human Rights of 1950 was incorporated into British law as the Human Rights Act of 1998. It is true that Britain adhered to the Convention previous to this time, but British citizens had first of all to seek satisfaction in the British courts before being able to appeal to the European court if it seemed that their human rights had not been respected in the verdict of the national court. The passing of the Human Rights Act embodied the Convention's coherent set of statements about human rights into British law. This then allowed the interpretation of existing British laws and regulations in terms of human rights. Not only are the law courts affected, but every 'public authority', which includes government departments and agencies, local government, health authorities and a range of other bodies, has a duty to protect the rights set out in the law.

The article of the Human Rights Act that stands out immediately as being of the greatest possible relevance is Article 10, which states that:

> Everyone has the right to freedom of expression.

Some people would argue that for centuries before the Human Rights Act, the principle of freedom of expression was actually better protected in Britain by custom and usage than it was by the laws that were on the statute books of many other countries. However, it was obviously a weakness that only the exceptions to the principle (and every system of laws, including the American, includes exceptions to these freedoms) were fully set out in British law. For instance, over the years Britain has had a series of Official Secrets Acts (currently the 1989 Act is in force) that severely restrict the ability of government employees to exercise a right to freedom of expression in relation to their employment. The absence of any explicit statement of the principle in law meant that challenges to official secrets law and other aspects of the control of information in Britain were hard to maintain. The Human Rights Act has changed this, and now people can use it to bring cases in the courts for alleged violations of the right of freedom of expression (and, of course, the other rights in the Act). An early information-related example is the attempt by the serial killer Dennis Nilsen to assert a right to obtain homosexual pornography while in prison. He alleged in October 2001 that, while fellow prisoners were allowed heterosexual pornography, prison rules forbade the magazines that he wanted to obtain, and that this was a breach of his human rights.

The provision of information services by libraries and other institutions is clearly affected by arguments of this type. A 'public authority' providing public internet access is acting completely within the spirit and the letter of the Human Rights Act. In fact, you could argue that information services are now directly obliged to avoid anything (such as filtering internet access) that might conflict with the principle of freedom of expression. This raises the possibility of challenges in the courts to services that are alleged to be in the 'breach of statutory duty' by restricting freedom of expression. However, like all the rights in this and other statements of human rights, the right of freedom of expression is subject to some limitations. The Act specifically mentions limitations arising from national security, the protection of morals, and the licensing of media. To defend an action that someone brought against it, a public authority would have to show that what it had done in restriction of freedom of expression was the kind of exception that the law allows, and was in proportion to the problem it sought to correct. This principle of proportionality is likely be the substance of many cases under the Act, and providers of public internet access who intend to operate some form of restriction should think hard about whether it can be shown to be proportional to the threats allegedly presented by unrestricted access.

Freedom of information laws

Freedom of expression is almost entirely pointless without freedom of access. A government can grant its citizens a right to freedom of expression, but if it then denies them the right to listen to speeches and read publications, and does not allow expression of certain viewpoints in public media, the right would be effectively useless. But more than this, freedom of access to information means that there need to be structures actively facilitating access. In parts of the world, particularly the Nordic countries, there are long-established rights for citizens to examine official documents, and other countries have laws setting out the rights of citizens to information held by government and its agencies. The most prominent is undoubtedly the 1966

US Freedom of Information Act. This provides a robust mechanism for access. Under this law any citizen can write to a government agency requesting full disclosure of information on any topic on which he or she believe the agency has files, without demonstrating any 'need to know'.

A number of other countries also have freedom of information legislation. Australia, for instance, has its Freedom of Information Act, 1982. Canada has a Charter of Rights and Freedoms as part of the Constitution of 1982, which protects 'freedom of thought, belief, opinion and expression' and is backed by an Access to Information Act. In France, there is a law of July 1978 on Access to Administrative Documents, a law of January 1979 ensuring the right of access to public archives, and a law of July 1979 requiring the administration to justify refusals of access to information.

Freedom of Information Act

In November 2000 Britain joined the list of countries that have a Freedom of Information Act. However, this disappointed many of those who had hoped for a strong, clear measure. It only seems to cover a rather narrow range of possibilities because of the wide ranging exceptions that are allowed. It has yet to be tested in the courts so judgement must, to some extent, be reserved. Once the British law comes fully into force (which will not be until 2005) it will give people the right of access to information held by public authorities and this will effectively extend people's existing rights of access to information about themselves under data protection law (see next section) to other categories of information. It will be administered by an Information Commissioner, who will also deal with the existing data protection law. The Commissioner will promote good practice on access to information among public authorities, and this is intended to create an improved access environment generally. This is likely to be helpful in relation to internet access because it will provide a strong statement in favour of the principle of access. It goes along with the practice of making government reports and other documents available on the internet. Where this is done, for instance by the American federal government, it is a massive contribution towards establishing the medium as a freedom of access area. Britain also makes considerable amounts of important documentation available in this way, for instance via the website opengovernment.gov.uk. Alongside these positive steps, British law now offers the possibility of challenges to restrictions on access to information both through the Information Commissioner and through actions under the provisions of the Human Rights Act.

Privacy

Privacy law

Many countries have laws on personal privacy, but until the Human Rights Act Britain had none. That has now been changed by Article 8, which states that:

> Everyone has the right to respect for their private and family life, their home and their correspondence.

What the Human Rights Act did by stating a right of privacy was to make possible a tort of breach of privacy in British law. As I mentioned earlier, a tort is a kind of wrong done to someone, which is not a criminal offence, but which can be set right and compensated for in the civil courts. Torts include breach of confidence, but, until now, not breach of privacy. Breach of confidence does deal with private information. It is concerned with the harm created by the misuse of private information that has been shared in some way with another (usually, but not always, between employer and employee). Private things that had not been shared in confidence were previously not protected. However, since the Human Rights Act was passed, the courts have heard some claims for breach of privacy. The model Naomi Campbell objected to revelations in a newspaper about aspects of her private life, and the actor Michael Douglas and his wife, the former Catherine Zeta Jones, sought to prevent the magazine *Hello!* from publishing photos of their wedding without permission. By listening to this kind of action the court effectively created a new tort. It is not actually necessary to have an Act of Parliament to set out the details of this, as the courts can form judgements based on the time-honoured principles that apply across this area of the law.

Data Protection Law

What Britain has had for some years, in common with all the states of the European Union, is data protection law. The Data Protection Acts of 1984 and 1998 provide that every holder of files of information about people must manage those files according to a set of rules and give access to the people with whom the files are concerned. These rules provide that the information must be kept confidential and only used for the purposes for which it was collected. The individuals to whom the information refers must be given access to it, if they ask, and they have the right to challenge the content of this information if they feel it is inaccurate or should not be held. Data protection laws such as this are now to be found in very many countries, and they are a recognition that the storage of personal data, whether on paper or computerized, is a considerable threat to the privacy of the individual. But it is the ease with which computerized records can be accessed, manipulated and transferred elsewhere, including to other countries, that has induced countries to pass this type of legislation. These laws are of considerable significance to public institutions as holders of personal data about their clients. Internet use involves the automatic creation of electronic files about users in the computer system, and there are many websites that contain files of personal data, so institutions need policy on data protection in relation to the internet as a matter of quite high priority.

Anti-privacy laws

Britain also has an increasing number of what might be called anti-privacy laws that affect internet users, particularly in relation to their use of e-mail facilities. Perhaps the most striking example of this tendency is the Regulation of Investigatory Powers Act, passed in July 2000. This is explicitly aimed at updating the law on the interception of communications to take account of technological change such as the growth of the internet. Among its other provisions, it requires that internet service providers include a 'reasonable interception capability' in their networks. If officially intercepted communications are encrypted, suspects can be made to divulge the decryption keys on pain of imprisonment. Although this does not explicitly concern the providers of access (as opposed to 'service providers') it represents an official commitment to placing responsibility for disclosure of information that might well be confidential much closer to service organizations like libraries.

More specifically, the Lawful Business Practice Regulations (which derive their force from the Regulation of Investigatory Powers Act) give employers the right to monitor workplace communications without consent. This is so that they can detect activities such as misuse of the internet, and fraud in particular. Of course this is important to the employer because it effectively endorses surveillance to limit personal usage of office e-mail, and to ensure that work standards and contractual requirements are met. All the employer has to do is give notice that employees may be subject to monitoring. This is no idle threat. Companies in many parts of the world already do this and there have been many instances of the disciplining and sometimes dismissal of employees on the basis of intercepted communications. Thus, the legislative tendency in Britain is to remove aspects of institutions' discretion to decide on what they consider are the ethical solutions to data problems. Then it provides institutions with powerful legal tools that can be used to control what their employees do with data. Again, this may not affect the relations of public internet access providers with their users, but it does create an atmosphere relating to internet communication which cannot help but be reflected in public provision.

Harassment

Harassment is becoming quite frequently mentioned as an offence committed both via the internet (persistent unwelcome e-mail messages, for instance) and by the way the internet is used in public institutions (display of pornography or other offensive material). This may be a difficult concept, but the law now does recognize that there are offences against the individual of an intrusive, disturbing and threatening nature that fall short of actual physical violence and molestation. These are essentially offences against the mind and have been recognized more readily in the US courts than in those of other countries. In British law this offence is recognized by the Protection from Harassment Act of 1997, but the Criminal Justice and Public Order Act 1994 could also apply. Harassment in public internet access would involve persistent and malicious use of images and other material from the internet to cause distress. This could mean distress to another user or a member of staff in an institution that provides public access.

Already several American library users and librarians have claimed that they have been harassed by the behaviour of some internet users. What is more, they have claimed that their distress was such that they ought to receive not only better protection against this in future (presumably by the application of filtering software), but that they should also have substantial financial compensation for what they have already suffered. A female employee of Chicago Public Library alleged in 2001 that her exposure to internet pornography viewed by the library's users created a hostile work environment and that her complaints to the library administration were ignored. Her action was filed with the US Equal Employment Opportunities Commission on the grounds that this constituted sexual discrimination. She argued that her employers should have protected her, and other women, from exposure to actions (blatant and intimidatory display of pornography) almost exclusively committed by men. Even in other countries less litigious than the USA there is also a strong likelihood of this type of claim emerging. Indeed the employees of Dublin Public Library in Ireland have threatened to boycott public internet access service because they felt exposed to harassing experiences as a result of the use of pornography by the public (Willson and Oulton, 2000). Significantly, in this case, as in others, on examining the records of thousands of instances of use it was discovered that the number of visits to pornographic sites by Dublin's users was tiny. The important point was that cases, when they did occur, were distressing to an extent that made their infrequency seem rather irrelevant to those affected.

Action by someone against a user who they felt had harassed them in this way is also conceivable under British law. This would certainly involve the institution that provided access in some time-consuming and expensive work in collecting and providing evidence for the lawyers handling the action, and possibly unpleasant appearances in court to give evidence. This would be bad enough, but there is also a direct threat to any institution that might seem to permit harassment of this kind. Providing unfiltered or insufficiently supervised access might well be taken as taking insufficient care to prevent something like this happening, when it ought to have been identified as a threat and precautions put in place. There is a genuine possibility here of action of some kind by a user against a library or other institution on the grounds that it was broadly responsible for what had taken place. In Britain this would probably fall short of legal action against the institution, but assuming that this would be so might be very risky. For instance, members of staff in a British institution who felt themselves insufficiently protected against harassment by users might very well take their case to an employment tribunal.

Obscenity

Obscenity laws

Most of the user-related problems with the internet arise from the presence of content that is arguably obscene. In theory, the laws on obscenity should make it possible to prosecute those responsible and thus bring the problem to an end. However it is not so straightforward in practice. Obscenity is very definitely in the eye, or ear, of the beholder. What is art or poetry to one person is often obscenity to another, and the laws have the most terrible difficulties in coming up with definitions that will stand the test of exposure in the courts. The content of mainstream newspapers, television and cinema is now far more liberal than seemed possible 40 years ago, and specialist publications and videos push the limits a great deal further. The generally acceptable sticking point seems to be pornography involving children, though various extreme sexual practices would also fall outside the limits tolerated by the majority.

Standards of what is acceptable also vary strikingly from country to country. In Britain newsagents place magazines with 'adult' content on the 'top shelf', out of the reach of children (and small adults, it should be pointed out). This contrasts with the kiosks of other countries where magazine covers with photographs of models revealing their genitalia are openly displayed. There is even great variation of practices and standards within some countries: states of the USA, for instance, can be very different from each other on matters of obscenity. In Britain, legal control of publications and videos on grounds of obscenity is exercised under the 1959 Obscene Publications Act. The Act effectively founders on its definition of obscene as something likely 'to deprave or corrupt'. No one feels sufficiently confident of what this means to make it effective as a legal test, especially in an age when people generally feel confident of their own, and others', ability to contemplate extremes of sexual and other conduct without risk of corruption. However, the 1978 Protection of Children Act and the 1988 Criminal Justice Act are also relevant. Both have been used to prosecute people accused of storing, disseminating and downloading sexual content, particularly child pornography.

Regulation of content

Parallel to the legal restrictions, Britain has a system for the classification of films and videos. This is administered by the British Board of Film Classification (formerly the British Board of Film Censors), an industry body, whose classifications are not enforceable in law. Nevertheless, the film distributors, cinemas, video shops and broadcast TV channels all pay at least token respect to the age limitations that the classifications suggest. Other countries have different patterns of legal provision to address obscenity, although they tend to rely on mixtures of licensing, pre-censorship and laws to enable the prosecution of producers of material that does appear on the market. The internet as a medium that does not respect borders reflects all of these varieties of practice which means that, in effect, it is open to content that is obscene in some jurisdictions but not in its place of origin. This messy legal situation is something that has to be faced by providers of public internet access. The dilemma is that they are obliged to provide a service that is legal according to the laws of their own country, while using a medium that recognizes absolutely no distinction based on the geographical origin of content.

Defamation

Internet content that is harmful to someone, usually because it is incorrect, might well be actionable in law. Whether it is legally actionable or not, such information is something that no responsible information service will want its users to consult and, particularly, risk trusting. In neither case is there much danger of action against the provider of public internet access, though it might just be conceivable if the institution gives the content a positive endorsement that later proved to be inappropriate. The real danger is that of the annoyances and bad publicity that might come from association of any kind with a case brought against the originators of damaging content.

Defamation is perhaps the most obvious example of harmful content. Defamation is defined as communicating a statement that tends to lower someone in the eyes of other members of society. Statements of this kind are rife on the internet. People feel free to express strong sentiments in newsgroups and on discussion lists. There have been some examples of actions taken in the courts by people and institutions who have felt themselves libelled. For instance, in 1997, Western Provident, an insurance company, obtained £450,000 damages from Norwich Union, a rival company. Norwich Union had circulated untrue statements about Western Provident's alleged financial problems in the form of internal e-mails, that in turn created damaging rumours.

This is good enough reason for professionals involved in running intranets, providing website content, or just communicating by e-mail, to be cautious of what they and colleagues say. However, they are most unlikely to be considered responsible for the content of a libel that they themselves did not originate. The chief danger would come if they failed to remove defamatory material on some service that they themselves were providing if its presence had been drawn to their attention. Similarly the general liability of public institutions for defective information is not usually a legal problem. Unless the information is specifically given in response to an enquirer and effectively vouched for by the provider, there is no scope for action in the courts by an injured party. Information services provided free of charge (or that do not involve some form of mutual obligation as the equivalent of a charge) will not fall under the law of contract, and claims for negligence in providing free-of-charge information would be hard to maintain. However, this is not in any way a reason to feel free of responsibility for harm that might result from content obtained via the service. At the very least it would attract unfavourable comment if the institution were to be involved in any way with a dispute over alleged harm suffered from information.

Intellectual property
Intellectual property on the internet

As an information professional you will be well aware of the provisions of the main national intellectual property law in your own country, such as the Copyright, Designs and Patents Act of 1988 in Britain or the US Copyright Act of 1976. The concept of fair use, or fair dealing, allows some exceptions to the copyright rules on behalf of users of libraries and other information institutions. Despite this the laws are hard for information professionals to police on behalf of the rights holders, because users have little respect for the concept and practices of copyright. Bodies such as the Copyright Licensing Agency (CLA) and Newspaper Licensing Agency in Britain and their various sister bodies in countries throughout the world, are the interface between the rights holders and information professionals. These 'collecting societies' are extremely active in asserting the rights of their members but information professionals have established effective working relationships with them over the years.

Today, however, an intellectual property conflict is taking place at a global level, with the internet as the main zone of conflict. When content is made available over the internet, even the basic traces of acceptance of the intellectual property concept tend to vanish and people feel free to take and use what they want as if it were a common good in which they have a share by right. This places the onus very firmly on the owners of intellectual property rights to come up with ways of protecting their property. This is a responsibility that they have proved very willing to take on. One of the ways they have done it is to shift payment for intellectual property products from a single payment for purchase, to payments for licences. Licence payments take many forms, including both regular subscriptions allowing unlimited use of specified kinds, through to payment per instance of usage. This has meant a major adjustment on the part of information institutions from a culture of purchase to a culture of licensing. Up until recently legislation has failed to keep pace with this.

New legislation

In the USA there is recent legislation, the Digital Millennium Copyright Act of 1998, which is chiefly designed to prohibit the circumvention of the technical means that rights holders might use to protect their property rights from infringement (mainly over the internet). The European Directive on the Harmonisation of Certain Rights in the Digital Environment, passed in 2001, is a much more fundamental attempt to bring the law up to date. Essentially it seeks to move intellectual property law into a licensing regime, in contrast to the emphasis in older law on the outright sale of intellectual property. Both of these new measures naturally have considerable implications for public institutions that license intellectual property on behalf of their users. European library and information bodies lobbied hard during the Directive's process of adoption. This lobbying seems to have been rather successful in retaining the scope for public access to copyright works over the internet. Member states do have considerable discretion as to the way in which they apply the Directive, but libraries and other information institutions are given exemptions in rather the way they were under previous legislation. For instance, users will be able to download content for private use, but the authorities in each country will have to decide whether they will have to pay for this. Therefore, as far as can be seen in the months immediately after the Directive came into force, it preserves the situation in which information professionals hold a kind of balance between rights holders and users. This isn't a particularly enviable position, however, when intellectual property is in the kind of turmoil described in Chapter 2.

Conclusion

Awareness of the law is obviously important, but I would suggest that the most important reasons for awareness include the following.

- A knowledge of the law is an essential element in devising and putting in place good systems and procedures for the management of access and advising users on what is genuinely acceptable and what is not.
- It also makes a great deal of sense to know the law so that you can avoid involvement in cases concerning others. Having to collect and provide documentation for an investigation can be difficult and time consuming, and the prospect of any kind of court appearance is extremely stressful to most people. Of course, when it has to be done, either to protect someone who is in danger of penalties they may not deserve, or to ensure that a verdict is brought against someone who has been acting illegally, then it has to be done well.
- An awareness of the law is important to show the boundaries between the domains of law and ethics for the purposes of making decisions. Of course, these overlap. A law will very often arise from precisely the same principles that are invoked in ethical decision making and the law may help in drawing useful distinctions, such as what is harmless mischief and what is activity that is actually damaging to the extent that it needs to be prevented by the setting of penalties.
- At the same time, knowledge of what the law actually says will make it possible to identify if and when laws are unsatisfactory when looked at from the standpoint of professional ethics (or, indeed, simple practicality). A professional does need to have a clear understanding of the possibly conflicting demands of law and principle and it is a mistake to view law as above criticism or beyond change.

References

Armstrong, C. J. (ed.) (1999) *Staying legal: a guide to issues and practice for users and publishers of electronic resources*, London, Library Association Publishing.

Nelson, N. (2001) Legal and liability issues related to internet access, *Library Administration and Management*, **15** (1), 14–16.

Smith, G. (ed.) (1996) *Internet law and regulation: a specially commissioned report*, London, FT Law and Tax.

Willson, J. and Oulton, T. (2000) Controlling access to the internet in UK public libraries, *OCLC Systems and Services*, **16** (4), 194–201.

5
Managing internet access

Ethics and the law provide two necessary approaches to handling the management of public internet access facilities, but there is also a practical management dimension. Naturally this includes all the initial decisions over financing a service, procurement of equipment and other basic matters. You will have realized that virtually everything that I am saying in this book starts from the assumption that initial financial and equipment issues have already been dealt with. This is not a book about how to justify a service to funding bodies or how to plan the technical aspects of it. It is about how to run a service that people can use with a sense of assurance.

The chapter begins with a brief coverage of practicalities, focusing on: types and levels of service; siting of service areas; and staffing and supervision levels. The other issues dealt with in the chapter fall under the following headings:

- Computer service aspects (the practical means by which facilities are provided and maintained)
- Staff training
- Registration of users
- User instruction and assistance
- Supervision (the handling of public access facilities so that things go smoothly for users)
- Monitoring, filtering and blocking.

Internet access services in practice

It is important that new services be set up with a good policy framework in place, but the current need is just as much for a sorting out of ideas in the very many existing services where policy is incoherent and confused. My intention is to discuss managing access in a way that will be useful in either case – both where access is about to be offered to the public, and where it is already being offered. The basic issues ought to be properly thought through when the original decision to provide a service is made, but there is plenty of reason to believe the detail is often neglected and dealt with in a series of more or less ad hoc decisions. Although I mentioned statistics of how many public access services are in place or planned in government policy in an earlier chapter, there is a lack of baseline data on how provision is handled by different institutions. This makes it rather unsafe to generalize about the current approaches to dealing with internet access provision. However, a few indicators based on personal observation at various institutions will give an idea of the types of things that are done.

Types and levels

Internet access services vary a good deal according to the type of institution providing the facilities. By and large, museums, archives and other specialized institutions only provide internet access points so that users can pursue their studies by using relevant content that is available from beyond the walls of the institution. Usage that is not relevant to the subject field is either directly prohibited or only allowed or ignored as a kind of courtesy to users. Likewise educational institutions usually make it clear that internet access is not provided for non-educational purposes. At the same time they tolerate high levels of personal use as a matter of goodwill to their students and staff. All of this usually involves service points that are there for any member or authorized visitor and that offer a standard, complete internet service. This may also include access to the institution's own digital resources and facilities (such as a library OPAC) on the same machines, but these local facilities are often offered separately on non-internet machines.

When a general, multipurpose service is offered, as in public libraries, it is pretty common to have different types of facilities for different purposes and different sectors of the public. This may be partly something that has grown out of the piecemeal digital services with which many institutions began. It also reflects a sense that there are different needs in the community that call for different types and levels of service. The two most obvious aspects of this are services to children and young people, and more intensive services for users who are prepared to pay for more time at the terminals or extra facilities like access to software packages. Services to children can include homework clubs, with helpers to provide guidance at the times when the terminals will be used, and dedicated services where access is through a gateway or portal that directs young users to selected sites that are felt to be of particular value and appropriateness. A cruder version of this is children's service points that are merely heavily filtered so as to provide a 'safe' service that will not worry parents. Types of services for the general public (including children and young people in some places) can be in any of the following forms:

- beginners' services supervised by a member of staff who can give some basic guidance
- casual services available with minimal formalities, for specified periods (e.g. half an hour) at busy times, with use for e-mail a major purpose
- 'research' services with bookable machines, possibly access to local facilities including CD-ROMs, and possibly no e-mail access
- services linked to facilities for formal computer-user courses, possibly provided by an outside organization
- open learning facilities with access to teaching packages in addition to internet facilities.

There is a quite complicated mix of influences governing what your institution might actually offer out of these and other possibilities. Influencing factors include an assessment of demand, not just in terms of numbers of people likely to be interested, but the types of people (students, businesspeople, older users and hobbyists, experienced or inexperienced, wanting full facilities or mainly needing communication facilities, etc.). Government and local government policies, particularly in terms of subsidies and support offered, set important parameters. There is also the appropriateness of particular types of service to the institution's other services and facilities.

Location

The location of services in the building will naturally depend to some extent on just what is possible (space and connection facilities available) but accessibility to different types of users, and potential for supervision, for whatever reason, are important. There is no fundamental reason why a public internet access facility should not be in some area or building totally detached from the institution's other facilities, if that is the most convenient alternative. There is an obvious distinction between what might be right for a casual or beginners' facility (siting at entrance level with possible proximity to entrances or street windows, and general visibility from busier areas) and what might be needed for research-type facilities (a quieter, less frequented area, possibly on another floor of the building). A service for which users pay, and one that is provided on the basis of bookings for terminals, may also need to be located in an area quickly accessible to staff who have other responsibilities in addition to supervising the internet access point.

Staffing

What it is very important to say about staffing of public internet access is that supervision is always necessary at some level or other. It must definitely be taken into account in staffing provision, and it must be admitted that providing a new service like internet access is likely to increase the need for staff rather than decrease it. Many of the difficulties that have been experienced with public internet access, and many of the difficulties that are fearfully anticipated, exist because this type of service has been treated as if it would create nil or minimal staffing requirements. In turn, much of the debate over filtering takes place because it is assumed that an automated way of dealing with unacceptable use is necessary because human supervision will not be available. The staffing demands of internet provision may not be high if users are mainly experienced and if a certain level of trust is extended to them, but the demands are still there. Other types of internet access provision, such as services to children, require predictably high levels of staffing. This may be an unpalatable suggestion when funds for public services are so constrained, but it still has to be made.

Computer service aspects

The computer professional's approach

The actual provision of services on a day-to-day basis requires technical skills and know-how. This is not something that information professionals can usually offer at the levels necessary to keep a public internet access service running effectively. Breakdowns, upgrades of hardware and software, security problems and other considerations of this kind, all call for specialist input. This is usually provided by a computer services department, located either within the service department (library, information centre, museum, or whatever) or separate and giving a general service to a number of different departments. Whatever the particular setup in your institution, it is important to be conscious of the fact that computer services are provided by people with different backgrounds, training, attitudes and professional agendas to those of information professionals. This usually means that there is a need for close liaison and careful specification of needs, but it can sometimes amount to a clash of cultures.

At the risk of being inaccurate and very unfair I would suggest that the overwhelming preoccupations in computer services are technology and systems. A relish for hardware and/or software with all their facilities, intricacies and quirks is a necessary requirement for a computer service professional. A strong concern for the systems that the computers serve follows naturally from that. Developing systems, keeping them running and protecting them from intrusion or disaster are all things that we can expect computer services professionals to be good at and enthusiastic about. True, they may also be interested in content, but the tendency is for them to see content as someone else's concern. In contrast, I would characterize the information professional's culture as based on concern for content and users, in that order. I personally think that it should be the other way round, with users first and content a close second, but whichever way you think it works, the priorities are rather different from those of computer services personnel.

I would also suggest that computer services tend to have an idealized and rather detached view of the users of their systems. In their version, users are people who will appreciate and gain value from what is so lovingly provided for them (by the computer and software industries, by systems developers and by computer services departments). They will not be demanding and ungrateful individuals who want systems that serve their own (perverse and unimaginative) needs and who persist in ignoring the wonderful things that are actually on offer. My defamatory and partisan account of things could be supported by anecdotal evidence, but it is probably better just to say that the real point is to remember that agendas do not necessarily coincide, and that this calls for careful planning, specification of needs, and negotiation. With forethought the two professional approaches can be made to complement each other very effectively.

Security

One enormously valuable contribution that computer services bring to provision of public internet access points is their concern with the security of systems. Handbooks like Shim, Qureshi and Siegel (2000) set out to help computer professionals provide systems that will be as secure as possible against theft, sabotage, data and system errors, and disasters like fire and flood. The task of the service manager is even more difficult in the internet age, when computers cannot be totally isolated for purposes of protection against the dangerous and risky things that outside users may do accidentally or deliberately. Computer security can involve technical solutions (detection devices and automatic shut-off systems, elaborate backup provision, etc.), but much more important than these in the long term are good staff practices and procedures.

Identifying and implementing good security practices and procedures calls for good organizational policies that set out the organization's computer service priorities. Then computer service managers can identify and evaluate risks, install control systems, prepare contingency plans and monitor the performance of systems in relation to the plans. This should ensure that information professionals and users have a system that actually works when they need it. The downside of the computer security process is that it naturally identifies users as one of the threats to system security. This can lead to a preference for controlling, and even authoritarian solutions to user-related problems. Managed badly this can mean less effective and satisfactory information service to users. Managers of public access to the internet should never let themselves assume that what is good for systems is best for the organization. Once this assumption starts to govern policy and practical decisions then it is likely that service to users will be damaged.

Staff training

General skills

No aspect of service is likely to work effectively without well-trained staff, and administration of public internet acess points is no exception to this. Some of the training that is relevant is no different from what staff should receive for any public service function. Customer care, including good manners, procedures to make sure that user enquiries and requests come to satisfactory results, and ways to handle complaints and challenges, is vital. In particular staff will need basic administrative skills, so as to be able to manage fair access to terminals. Staff themselves will need training ability, so that they can help users develop their skills at the point of use. They may also need training in the delivery of formal instruction to groups, if that is part of the way in which the institution believes that it should help users. Staff should also be given opportunities to become knowledgeable about the internet and the WWW so as to be able to help users construct the best search strategies. A proportion of the training that all of this calls for can be delivered by the institution itself, either on the job or in more formal training packages. However, the more advanced and specialized aspects will be provided best by using programmes and one-off sessions put on by professional associations, colleges, training companies and commercial service providers.

Supervisory skills

What is utterly vital is that training should include thorough attention to dealing with the difficult situations that arise out of the presence of illegal and disturbing content on the internet. I discussed harasssment as a legal issue in Chapter 4, but use and misuse of content is fundamentally an ethical issue. The ethical question here is 'Should staff be obliged to deal with content that may be shocking and disgusting, or offensive to their own personal beliefs?' This is difficult to answer, but generally it is expected professionals will put their own views and preferences on one side when providing a service for the public.

However, if we reframe the question as 'Should staff be obliged to provide service to people who use content deliberately or carelessly in a way that causes offence to others?', the answer is more clearly 'No'. There is a difference between access and the misuse of access. Someone might well want to look at material with extreme sexual, racist or other offensive content for a variety of reasons, many of which might generally be considered valid. If they were to do that discreetly, they would be using their freedom in a way that is consistent with the essential principle. Gratuitously flaunting this use in front of others would be a different matter. Disgusting and disruptive behaviour is something that occurs in all sorts of public places and it does not have to be tolerated. Specifically, it does not have to be tolerated even in an institution devoted to free expression and free access to information.

Making the distinction between what is legitimate exercise of a freedom and what is antisocial behaviour or harassment is not easy. Acting upon a judgement of this kind is probably even less easy. Dealing with disruptive users has not been common content in training programmes for information professionals, though the case for its inclusion in training is probably stronger than it ever was. Society has a genuine problem in how to deal with disruptive behaviour of all kinds. The staff of public services can be put in various kinds of danger when they have to confront people who are behaving antisocially, whether that is on a bus, in an office or shop, a public library or anywhere else. The managers of any institution generally are failing their staff if they do not train them in dealing with this kind of thing. Managing internet public access is far from the most dangerous and confrontational arena, but the same principles apply here as in more high-risk areas. Staff need to know what they are expected to do, what they should say to disruptive users, and the fallback and safety procedures that are in place when situations deteriorate and become especially hard to handle.

Registration of users

Joining procedures

The administration of access facilities is tidiest if users are registered or enrolled as members of the organization, but the question of 'signing up' for internet service is a delicate one. Many institutions do require people to take out a membership card for internet use, either as part of a broader membership, or for this type of service as a separate facility. The membership form, and maybe the card itself, is likely to carry a formal acceptance of rules and regulations, and the sanctions and penalties associated with breaking them. For instance, this has long been the normal way for libraries to introduce their rules for the return of borrowed items and fines for non-return. However, there are differences in the type of registration required between a free internet access service and one for which payment is required.

With a free service there is the option of eliminating joining procedures altogether. Some institutions prefer that at least part of the service is on this extremely informal basis. After all, library users who just wish to consult material within the library have generally been able to do so without having to reveal their identity. Some people, for perfectly good reasons, prefer this anonymity and would prefer that it be extended to information seeking on the internet. Therefore, in the interests of inclusiveness and so as not to put off vulnerable members of the community (asylum seekers and people with histories of mental problems have been mentioned to me as examples) some institutions keep 'membership' formalities to a minimum or dispense with them entirely. This may involve no contact at all with staff, as the user may just take the next available workstation and begin to use it. The disadvantage of this is that no real agreement will have been established on the terms under which the service is used.

If membership of some kind is required for a free service, it has the advantage that the institution can use the joining procedure to sign people up to its policy on internet use, and to obtain tacit agreement to its procedures. The attraction of this is that signing up creates a kind of 'contract' between the service and the user as to how access will be used. This can be used to set out basic matters such as booking procedures, length of time online allowed if there are people waiting, whether downloading and printing are allowed and so on. By making procedures well understood from the very beginning a great deal of unnecessary and sometimes unpleasant dispute can be eliminated.

If internet facilities, or any other services, are provided in return for payment then the emphasis changes considerably. The agreement with the user becomes a contract in reality as well as in spirit. In this case the statements that are made to the user become the terms and conditions of the contract, and it is essential that they are set out in a clear and unambiguous way. Although it is highly unlikely that it would come to that, the agreement is enforceable in law. If it does no more, this strengthens a disgruntled user's bargaining power a great deal. With paid-for services it is absolutely essential that what is being offered is utterly clear, and that the rules and regulations applying to it are communicated effectively to the user.

Rules and regulations

Choosing the method by which rules and regulations are presented to the user is also important in relation to free services, and even to services that are provided on the totally informal basis mentioned above. The way in which it is done also makes statements about how strongly the institution is committed to what the policy says. The chosen method of presenting policy to users should make it easy for them to refer back to what the policy includes, or for staff to refresh their memory in cases of dispute. Mere oral mention of rules when a user first uses the service is not adequate for this purpose. There are three main ways by which policies can be more formally delivered to the user:

- handed over in the form of a leaflet when the user either joins or, in less formal systems, first uses the service
- displayed as a poster on the walls or partitions of a public access area, or attached in some way to the desks or terminals
- displayed onscreen, either each time a user accesses the system, or just on the first occasion (with a clear route back to the statement for reference purposes).

I have seen all of these in operation, and on some occasions the first two have not been very efficiently administered. I have found staff who cannot locate copies of the policy document to hand to an enquirer and others who had not noticed (and more worryingly, did not seem to have been told about) a poster carrying the policy that was displayed in the area.

For sheer efficiency, a policy that appears onscreen is the preferable alternative. The policy is not easily forgotten or ignored if it can be brought up onscreen at the press of a button. This contrasts with the ease with which users can mislay a piece of paper that has been handed to them, or ignore a poster among the (possibly irrelevant, and sometimes out-of-date) pieces of information cluttering up the walls of the service area. In some institutions, every time users log on to the public terminals the policy is displayed onscreen and they are effectively required to renew their commitment to it before being allowed to go any further with their session. Some institutions actually require the user to reaffirm acceptance of the policy each time they use the facilities. This may seem to be a rather oppressive way of handling the situation and it has to be asked whether it is more likely to encourage users to respect the ground rules than if a lighter touch were to be used. Nevertheless, the alternative is there, and some institutions feel it is a suitable way to handle things.

User instruction and assistance

User instruction, as it used to be provided in libraries, was often deeply dull and not particularly relevant to user interests. It could take an almost coercive form that sought to channel users into accepting information professionals' ways of doing things (right or wrong). It often sounded like 'This is the way you *should* use the catalogue' or 'Here is what you *must* do to find information in reference books'. We have largely moved away from this, and the emphasis is much more on providing instruction with a light touch and giving support that is responsive to need. This is the approach that is needed to help users of public internet access get the best out of the service. I stressed earlier that users of public internet access points are not necessarily there because they can't afford home access or do not have workplace or educational access. For some people, it is preferable to get their access along with some guidance in how to use it, the possibility of support (whether from other users or information professionals) when problems occur, and in a place with other different types of resources that they might want to use. They need to be able to find the support that they are looking for if they are to become the kinds of users who will encourage others to come and use the facilities.

Information literacy

The philosophy behind the kind of instruction that tends to be offered today is that of information literacy. The American Library Association developed a definition of information literacy as long ago as 1989. This says that information literacy is the ability to

> recognise when information is needed and have the ability to locate, evaluate, and
> use effectively the needed information.   (ALA, 2001b)

The treatment of information literacy by writers such as Bruce (1997) or Webber and Johnston (2000) places the types of instruction provided by libraries, or the training in IT skills that can be obtained from a variety of organizations in a much wider context. Information literacy includes ability to deal with the whole range of sources, real and virtual, and information literacy programmes seek to encourage not just skilful, but critical searching. The emphasis on evaluation and critical use of sources is particularly important because of the many ways in which internet content can be unreliable and misleading, as discussed in Chapter 2.

Portals

Creating a dedicated access route in the form of a gateway or portal can complement the good effects of information literacy programmes very effectively. A portal is the organization's own website, providing access to its own databases (a library's OPAC, for instance), and links into other websites selected for relevance and importance to users. It can also provide other facilities such as e-mail and search engines. The term vortal is also used, and this means a portal that provides information and services for a particular industry. The advantages that an institution can offer its users through well-designed and constantly updated portals are enormous. The services and resources can be tailored very closely to need and this also has the effect of directing attention away from internet content that may be less relevant or actually unwelcome. For an example of what this can look like, the American Library Association's *Resources for parents, teens and kids* (ALA, 2001a) provides guidance on how to use the internet safely and effectively, but, more importantly, it provides links to over 700 sites that have been selected for quality, interest and entertainment. This service is maintained by the ALA's Great Websites Committee so that it grows and changes with what is offered (and no longer offered) by content providers. An individual information institution is unlikely to be able to select and monitor as many sites as the ALA has done for links from its portal, but it can take advantage of the work of organizations like the ALA so as to offer assistance to its own users.

Supervision
Trust versus surveillance

When discussing supervision we need to acknowledge to ourselves that we think in terms of supervising facilities not only so that help is quickly at hand, but also so that control is possible. However, the need for control is not an inevitable conclusion when thinking about how to administer internet access facilities. Experienced users, particularly those with professional or educational motivation to use the facilities, can be offered trust. Facilities for a trusted user community can be placed in comparatively private and less obviously supervised areas of the premises. Certainly this is what is done in many institutions, where internet access may be in an area partially separate from other facilities. The idea is that this will be less disruptive for other users and professionals alike. It may seem to be a risk. Trust will certainly be betrayed on occasion, but on the other hand, treating people with respect often encourages responsible behaviour.

Reliable information on the scale of the problem of abuse of public internet access is scarce. Because when it occurs it is shocking and disturbing to staff there seems to be a tendency to exaggerate its frequency. There often seems to be a contradiction between what staff feel to have been the frequency, and what the system history shows to have been the case. For instance, a monitoring exercise at the Arizona State University libraries showed only a 1% rate of pornography use at the terminals (Konomos and Herrington, 2000). This would suggest that high levels of supervision are not required to deal with the problem of misuse. However, if supervision is minimized, there have to be procedures to enable response when breaches of trust do occur. Creating and administering these procedures can be a great deal less time consuming and expensive than creating systems of surveillance based on a fundamental attitude of mistrust.

If, however, close supervision is judged to be a necessity, the principles behind it need to be thought out. Until electronic surveillance became a possibility, it was the design of public areas that made supervision either easy or difficult. Where supervision was a priority, work space for the public was set out in open areas, often arranged so that what was happening was visible from a central point. Secluded alcoves and carrels did not form part of the design. Supervision might well be reinforced by staff walking around the work area at intervals to check that nothing unsuitable was going on. These methods are still used in institutions with rare and unique materials (research libraries, archives and museums particularly). Staff supervise closely to prevent theft, vandalism and accidental damage to materials.

In institutions where security for the materials is not an absolute priority, practice has generally moved away from suspicion as the guiding principle. In most academic libraries (other than research libraries), it is recognized that users need a mixture of public space and some more private space in which they can concentrate undisturbed when necessary. Then again, in information facilities where use is generally not for sustained periods, and resources are not particularly specialized (public libraries or school libraries, for example), private space may not be considered so important as an open, welcoming layout.

Layouts for internet access

Supervision is a key issue in deciding on layouts for internet access facilities. There are three key reasons why an area needs to be easily supervisable:

- First, if its users regularly ask for help, or obviously experience difficulties that they cannot overcome alone. This would definitely apply to children and other beginners, and possibly also to people making use of specialized content with inherent difficulties.
- Secondly, so as to protect the hardware from theft or damage. Theft of computer hardware, the chips in particular, has sometimes been so profitable that break-ins have occurred, and vandalism is always a possibility.
- Thirdly, because of a high level of disruption caused by users. This refers to the use of noisy and brightly flashing sites like computer games, but also to the use of sexual content and other disturbing forms of material that have been discussed in the previous chapter.

Supervising the facilities makes it possible to deal with users' need for help very effectively, and should also help to prevent theft and damage. The simplest way to achieve this is to have the workstations fairly close to the main staff desk, with the monitors easily visible, so that staff can see what is being used, if necessary. This type of arrangement also tends to discourage disruptive use of the facilities. However, it is not the only discreet method of dealing with the problem of disruption. The furniture and fittings that are chosen for the internet use area can provide an alternative, or complementary, answer to this.

Privacy screens have been used by some public access providers, for instance. These fit over the monitor and restrict the ability of anyone other than the user to view the screen. A similar effect can be achieved by the provision of headphones for private listening to audio material, and I have also seen the kind of goggles developed for virtual reality purposes provided in a public access area, with obvious benefits in keeping visual material private to its immediate user. Another variation on the screening-off of internet access workstations is to have the monitors recessed into the desk surface. Although some people like working with a monitor set up in this way it does have ergonomic disadvantages, requiring the user to adopt a working posture that is very unhealthy for any prolonged period. Workstations can also be placed in separate cubicles, or shielded from each other by the kinds of barriers that already divide the desk surfaces in many libraries. Such barriers could include some soundproofing material if thought necessary. None of these approaches is particularly satisfactory, however, and all of them tend to make it more difficult for staff to provide assistance to the user.

Disciplinary procedures

If the service is abused in some way and the rules are flouted, effective supervision leads to the implementing of disciplinary procedures. The way that these will be implemented needs be worked out properly in advance, so that staff know what is expected of them. It is vital that a system be applied consistently and fairly, and staff can only do this if they are well aware of the system that they are supposed to be applying. Warnings are the most appropriate first response to breaches of rules, but it needs to be clear how many and what type of warnings will be given before further procedures are applied. The next step can be depriving a user of service at the time when the infringement occurs, or for a specified period afterwards, or permanently. It needs to be clear at which staff level warnings can be given and penalties applied. There need to be procedures for recording actions of these kinds, and informing staff about what has been done. There also needs to be a means by which users can challenge penalties, and a system for reviewing decisions and the procedures under which they were made.

Application of monitoring, filtering and blocking

In earlier chapters I have discussed the group of processes that is usually referred to just as 'filtering' and also said something about the ethical aspects of the debate it has created. Here we need to look at it in management terms because it is, quite simply, the automation of processes that can otherwise be carried out by human beings. No doubt it seems natural to handle questionable aspects of the use of technology with a technological solution, but it isn't actually inevitable that you should do it this way. Like many technological solutions to human problems it has lower initial costs than dealing with it through the agency of human beings. Like other technological solutions it is also less sensitive, flexible and genuinely effective than human solutions, but that seldom stops managers turning to technology for solutions. It is important to remember that installing such software in a public information institution is a clear intrusion into the privacy of users. Therefore installation needs to be the result of a conscious ethical decision, and the legal implications, particularly data protection, should be carefully examined. This means that if you are going to use it, you need to make yourself aware of what filtering does and how it does it. Then you are in a position to choose a product that meets the needs of your service as closely as possible.

Choosing a filter

Making a good choice of filtering product is vital. Apart from the publicity material put out by suppliers of filtering products, there are also good numbers of product reviews available. Schneider (1997) is the most systematic, but Heins and Cho (2001) collates reports on 19 different products, including all the best-known ones. Schneider suggests a selection process that follows this sequence:

1 Identifying the network operating environment. This means finding out what will work with the existing hardware and software.
2 Making a needs assessment. Deciding whether a system is needed for some workstations only, or whether different levels of filtering will be needed for different parts of the service (children's and adults' services, for instance).
3 Identifying available products. The websites for different products can be located using search engines.
4 Discussions with vendors. This will be necessary to supplement the basic product information, investigate different versions of the product, and find out prices.
5 Testing products. Schneider stresses that this is by far the most important part of the process. It should be done with real use, at different settings, with as much professional and user group input as possible.
6 Making a decision. This should be based on careful comparison of products that meet the institution's criteria and should eliminate 'good' products that lack some essential feature.
7 Installing the product. The settings will need to be adjusted and readjusted according to experience.

Reviewing the use of filters

Once filtering is in place, it is important to realize that the responsibilities of the manager do not end with the choosing and installation of a particular system. Although it may seem on the surface as if the software handles everything, this is not the case. The blocking that takes place as a result of filtering also involves management decisions. No doubt, if you want to, you can just let a preset system block away according to the standards of someone working in the sofware house from which you bought your filtering product. To do this would, however, be a complete abdication of management responsibility. If your software is blocking pages and sites then you need to be able to answer for what it is doing. To be able to do this you need to be capable of altering the settings to meet the criteria your institution has adopted, or so as to react to cases that might be considered exceptional for one reason or another. Monitoring the operation of the software and responding to cases are both essential parts of using filtering systems. The final word on filtering, however, is that it should never be forgotten that choosing to use it is an ethical decision that goes against the tendency of decades of thinking and practice in the information professions. If you decide that you have to use it, make sure you use it carefully and responsibly.

Conclusion

The management of internet access is a contentious business. A glance at the professional press shows that stories about filtering and other aspects of managing access feature strongly among the issues discussed. My interpetation of this would be that first, internet access services are very new in most institutions, with even the best established only dating back for a few years. Their implementation has tended to be piecemeal. They have been sited wherever has been immediately convenient and supervised along with other services by staff with little or no special training. A view of the sort of rules that need to be applied has often been developed bit by bit, partially in response to the development of user demand and partially according to the experiences of staff in working with the services. However, I would suggest that the time for experimentation with services is largely over. Very soon they will be available in every information institution in developed countries as part of the normal range of what is offered. The need now is for coherent policies based on the knowledge we have of services in practice. The final chapter describes a policy-making process designed to help make this possible.

References

ALA (2001a) *Resources for parents, teens and kids*, available at
www.ala.org/parents

ALA (2001b) *Twenty first century literacy @ your library*, available at
www.ala.org/literacybrochure.html

Bruce, C. (1997) *Seven faces of information literacy*, Adelaide, Auslib Press.

Heins, M. and Cho, C. (2001) *Internet filters: a public policy report*, National
Coalition Against Censorship, available at
www.ncac.org/issues/internetfilters.html

Konomos, P. and Herrington, S. (2000) Evaluating the use of public PC
workstations at the Arizona State University libraries, *Electronic Library*,
18 (6), 403–6.

Schneider, K. (1997) *A practical guide to internet filters*, New York, Neal
Schuman.

Shim, J., Qureshi, A. and Siegel, J. (2000) *The international handbook of
computer security*, Chicago, Glenlake.

Webber, S. and Johnston, B. (2000) Information literacy: new perspectives
and implications, *Journal of Information Science*, **26** (6), 381–97.

6
Making a policy for public internet access

Up until this point in the book I have mainly been dealing with background matters and discussing the way things are now. This final chapter is intended as a guide to the creation of policies that might well change the way things are in your institution. Much of it comes in the form of checklists intended to be helpful when you are actually involved in making or administering policy.

First of all I deal with general issues related to policy within information institutions. I ask what a policy is, what it is supposed to do and to whom it is addressed. I then look at the qualities of a good policy. Next, and central to the chapter, I outline a process of policy making and implementation involving a series of distinct stages. Because of the importance and, to some extent, complexity of the research and consultation processes, I deal with each of these in more detail in separate sections, before going on to talk about the public documentation (the acceptable use policy or AUP) of the policy. The chapter concludes with a kind of 'quality control' checklist for your policy.

What is a policy?

The most obvious answer to the question 'What is a policy?' is that, in effect, it is what is represented by two types of document.

- One is for internal use and is likely to be full, detailed, supported by minutes of discussion and reports, and could be made even more explicit in a staff manual (see Appendix 3).
- The other type of documentation consists of short clear statements of the

essentials, intended for public consumption. The most common form this takes is an AUP, but specific aspects of policy (copyright or data protection, for instance) can be presented to the public in this way too (see Appendix 4).

But while these kinds of documentation are often referred to in a kind of shorthand as 'policy', in fact they are just the formal expressions of policy. A policy really consists of the agreed principles and intentions that guide the actions taken by some sort of body (ranging from an international organization, a state, a company, to a public sector organization such as a library, archive or museum). An individual can have a policy too, but we generally use the word to talk about corporate or communal policy. Policy exists as soon as there is some sort of agreement or consensus, whether this written down or not. It is based on a mutual understanding among those involved of what the organization stands for and what it is setting out to do. Teasing out precisely what an organization's policy is when the policy is not well documented can be a difficult task. Nevertheless, the policy is there and it is implicit in the activities of the organization: it is part of the organizational culture.

Implicit policy of this kind may seem to function quite effectively, particularly in small organizations such as partnerships, family businesses, or public institutions that have only a few committee members and staff. However, the problem is not just that an outside observer may misunderstand, but that members of the organization may misunderstand and policy may break down. Policy breakdown can easily occur when a rapid turnover of staff makes it hard to integrate new people into the organizational culture. What is more, policy is particularly vulnerable in the kinds of complex and fast-changing circumstances that require a great deal of fresh interpretation. The complexity of the 21st-century information world means that it is not very realistic for an organization, however small and personal, to continue without policy documentation. Therefore if someone told you that policy was something that existed because it was documented, they would not be entirely right, but what they said would make a lot of sense. I would suggest that any organization not only has a responsibility to develop good policy, but it also has a responsibility to document it well and make sure that the documentation is capable of reaching the appropriate people. This means that the most up-to-date and authoritative version should be available from a well-publicized single source.

Policy formation and documentation is particularly crucial for public internet access service, because it is such a difficult and contentious area. Journalists, lobbyists for particular viewpoints and politicians have contributed to some fairly hysterical commentary on the problems connected with the internet itself. While the controversy over public access points has seldom been as heated in Britain and other parts of the world as it has in the USA, there is still plenty of public anxiety over the suspected horrors and iniquities of what might be made available through publicly funded services. Policy making has to be done in the context of calls for legislation and more intensive policing, and demands that service-providing institutions effectively censor the access they provide. It is not possible to make these pressures go away unless institutions have effective policies that offer the 'access with assurance' that is the aim of this book.

What is policy supposed to do?

Properly worked-out policy has a great number of different uses. The most important ones in this context fall under the following headings.

Procedures

At its most basic, policy makes it possible to set out staff procedures in a way that makes for consistent and effective day-to-day management. If it is clear why the service is there and what it seeks to achieve, then the details follow logically. For instance, if a public library provides internet access with the aim of promoting social inclusion, it might concentrate on low-income families, older people and members of minorities. This would have immediate procedural consequences arising from decisions over the particular hours when service was provided, or the siting of the service point, that might differ quite strikingly from those implied by other policy priorities. Matters that could fall under this heading include:

- the line of responsibility for the service: who is responsible for what between managers, supervisory staff, technical staff, 'external' technical services
- the expectations as to how to deal with technical problems, and how unacceptable usage is defined and dealt with

- the procedures for booking terminals at busy times
- ways to deal with users who do not respect these arrangements
- services such as formal induction for groups of new users
- assistance routinely offered to new or infrequent users in terms of instruction and guidance
- ways to deal with users' requests for help
- methods for coping with frequently occurring problems.

Development

Policy should provide for coherent development of the service. Policy is not just about what you do today, it is about what you intend to do tomorrow. For instance, this might start with a broad intention to serve the maximum number of potential users who are members of an organization or who are residents of a particular area. This is fine as an initial policy objective, but it needs to be made a good deal more specific if it is to be useful. The ways to achieve this might include increasing the number of service points, increasing the number of terminals at existing service points, making the service more efficient so that more people could spend less time getting what they wanted from the same number of terminals, and various combinations of these and other alternatives. Policy involves decisions on the alternatives and setting out methods to achieve them.

Quality

It is policy that sets a framework for quality maintenance and enhancement. A baseline of values needs to be identified so as to enable the selection of indicators by which the quality of service can be measured. Statistics of performance can then be collected in a systematic and meaningful way. A service can be benchmarked against the statistics of the whole relevant sector, or against a few selected institutions that have particularly good and appropriate performance. If the indicators are well chosen and the statistics reliable, this should show how far quality is being maintained and improved. All of this depends, however, on the coherence that a clear policy gives to the exercise. Quality in terms of internet access provision means inputs such as amounts of money spent, number and up-to-dateness of terminals, hours of availability, and staff time devoted to the service. It also includes outputs such as the number of people using the service, the number and duration of sessions, amount of down time for the service, and the number of people receiving instruction and guidance. Measures of satisfaction gained from some device such as feedback forms complete the cycle. Policy puts the measurement in place and feeds it back into actions designed to meet broader policy objectives.

Agreement with users

Policy should create the basis of an agreement – a kind of 'contract' – with users. Any agreement has to be based on mutual commitments and responsibilities. On the part of the provider of public internet access that means specifying the level of service that it aims to provide. This sets the requirements that have to be placed upon the users (not to access pornography, to respect copyright, etc.) in a non-authoritarian context. This shows that it is reasonable to define the types of action that will be taken if users do not conform to what is required of them, i.e. the sanctions that might be taken against users who do not respect the agreement. Typical issues to be considered include:

- how complaints from users about other users, or about staff and the type of service they have received, will be dealt with
- the kind of action a supervisor is deputed to take (asking a user to stop using a particular site or type of site, depriving a user of access, reporting a user to a designated manager, etc.)
- how management will react to a reported case of this kind
- whether delinquent users will be allowed service in future, and under what circumstances they might be reported to the police or other authorities.

A service with a clear policy is in a position to make sure that users are not offered mixed messages, so that prompt and effective action can be taken when needed. This should have the effect of defusing difficulties (like alleged staff harassment, for instance) before they reach the level at which formal complaints by users or staff are made to outside authorities. In the event of such complaints being made, being able to cite a policy and report its enforcement according to prescribed procedures is likely to make the resulting process much easier to handle.

Assurance

This is a major effect and a major intention of policy. If the public feels that a service has clear, acceptable aims, it will generally offer its support. For example, there are the high levels of endorsement received by libraries when people are invited to respond to surveys of their approval of different public services. Even though fewer than 30% of the British population uses public libraries regularly, proportions in the high 90s express strong approval of libraries. This is partially because the public has virtually no grievances against libraries, in the way it might against housing departments, street cleaning or police. It is surely also because the public believes that it knows what public libraries stand for (very likely the education and self-improvement aspects rather than information and leisure) and that it approves of what it believes these purposes to be.

Properly set-out policy will also be conducive to user and staff confidence. By telling users and potential users what they can expect, and what is expected of them, a secure-seeming environment is fostered and people react well to this. Many staff are clearly less comfortable with internet access than other forms of information provision, and the main way that this is expressed is in the fear of harassment by users of pornography and other distasteful material. If staff know that they are not going to be obliged to put up with unacceptable behaviour, they will fear it less and have the confidence to get on with providing a good service.

Plausible denial

Policy that is explicit over what is permitted and what is not, and which sets out procedures for dealing with difficult situations makes these situations less likely. It also gives the institution a strong position in any dispute or formal enquiry process, such as a disciplinary committee, an employment tribunal or a court of law. Being able to say that something is not policy and, even better, that it is specifically forbidden or excluded by policy is a basis for 'plausible denial'. At its worst this is what is also known as covering your back (or covering your ass, in the USA) and is a means for trying to locate blame somewhere else. At its best it is only the beginnings of a defence, but it is a good beginning. What also has to be shown is that the policy has been widely made known, that procedures were in place to make it operate and that in the specific instance that is the subject of the dispute these procedures were followed. If none of these can be shown, the policy itself looks rather forlorn and is unlikely to produce much positive effect. Indeed if it seems to have been ignored, that might even be taken to show wilful neglect of precautions and responses that were known to be needed.

To whom is policy addressed?

Policy documentation is not just put together for its own sake. As should be obvious from the previous section, it addresses a readership. The readership is not, however, entirely homogenous: it consists of various groups of stakeholders. For policy to communicate to each of these groups as well as possible, their particular priorities and interests have to be borne in mind. These priorities and interests are likely to be sufficiently distinct from each other that one document will need sections addressing the concerns of different groups, and that more than one document may sometimes be required. When working on policy, it is important to have a clear idea of how the audience for policy documents should be segmented. The main stakeholders to be addressed when providing public internet access are the following.

Funders, administrators and regulators

In the first place, all policy documentation is addressed to those who pay for the service, or otherwise have the responsibility of vetting its fitness to be offered to the public. Funders include not only the government departments, local government authorities and other public authorities that provide the core budget for a service, but also a range of agencies, charities and trusts, other fund-raisers and corporate sponsors. The policy of an individual institution will need to conform to at least the broad outlines of national policy relating to its sector, and fit much more closely if it is to receive the grants and conditional contributions that form a large part of the funds that government makes available. It will also need to conform to the policy of a more immediate source of funding, such as a local authority, which might well be under different political control. Likewise, the other possible funders will also have their own 'political' agendas that policy may need to satisfy.

There will also be formal responsibilities to satisfy regulatory authorities, as for instance, the need for services offered by British public libraries to be approved by the UK Department for Culture, Media and Sport. The mission, aims and objectives of policy will all need to meet with approval at this level, but the requirements are likely to go much deeper. Service levels, matters of public safety, provision for particular groups (such as children or members of linguistic minorities) and many other aspects are very likely to be of strong interest to the service's paymasters and controllers.

The general public

It is important that policy conveys a message to the public, but the public does not have one set of needs, one opinion and one voice. Confident claims are always being made about the state of public opinion, but perception of what the public wants is filtered by the media, the political process and interest groups. What they say should not be taken entirely at face value. There is a tendency for a kind of 'moral panic' to be whipped up by those who have access to the media. This can fade away as soon as the next source of anxiety emerges, or it may touch on some fundamental and persistent concern that has a truer claim to be a part of public opinion.

We know that publicly expressed anxiety over internet content was at very high levels for the whole of the second half of the 1990s, but how deep and widespread a public concern did this represent? You may remember the hysteria in the summer months of 2001 caused by some very unpleasant incidents involving shark attacks on swimmers. In fact, shark attacks were not happening much more frequently than in previous years, it just seems to have been the case that they had been identified as a matter of immediate concern by the media. Although sharks in swimming areas are still a cause for concern, discussion of the issue vanished from the press and TV once bigger issues occurred (the destruction on 11 September 2001 of the World Trade Center in New York, for instance). The status of real concern over internet content may or may not prove to be genuinely measured by the amount of published and broadcast comment. As a contributor to policy making you need to make a critical reading of public comment so as to form a judgement as to how far it represents public opinion. This judgement may well be that there are a number of parallel strands of public opinion to which messages need to be addressed, rather than a single viewpoint.

Staff

Documents that address staff in ways that they understand and can work with are essential. Staff have to administer the policy and it is important they feel it makes sense. As far as possible, they should also feel that they own the policy that they are formally obliged to follow. You may have worked in a professional environment where consultation and communication with staff was not all it should be. If so, you will know how destructive this can be. It is true that not all policy can, or should be, based on staff consensus, but, if policy is to have a chance, information on it must be shared as effectively as possible. There must be answers to staff concerns in the documentation, even if some answers are not entirely palatable. At the very least, there must be clear policy lines that staff can understand and pass on to the public.

Individual users

As a policy maker, you will usually address the individual user in the form of an AUP rather than the more lengthy and elaborate documents directed to specific stakeholder groups. The content of the document is a selection and distillation of policy. It is designed to get clear messages over to people who do not want to spend a long time puzzling out what might be the practical implications of the organization's stated aims and objectives for internet public access. It is necessary to address the individual in this way because, as I implied in the last but one section, even a document that reflects public opinion is unlikely to fit comfortably with the preferences of all groups in society, let alone every individual.

There is an element of 'take it or leave it' about an AUP. It deals with the aspects of policy that need to be expressed as a set of rules, and states the consequences of not respecting these rules. This should not mean that the document is intimidating and likely to drive users away, merely that it should avoid confusion and ambiguity. The visual appearance of the document is important. Layout, typography, line length and other details can make a great deal of difference to the reception of a document. The tone needs to be friendly and positive precisely because users are the reason why the service is there in the first place. To risk antagonizing users through an over-emphatic statement of prohibitions would be a serious mistake. Documents should reaffirm that providing access is the intention and that prohibitions are as few and as lightly administered as possible.

Legal authorities

As I suggested earlier, there is always the possibility that some dispute or difficulty will bring the service under official scrutiny. This may even result in a case being examined in a forum such as an employment tribunal or court of law. As a matter of principle this should be avoided with the greatest possible energy. Good policy ought, as far as possible, to prevent the occurence of damaging disputes. It should specify clear follow-up procedures for when disputes do occur. These procedures ought to prevent disputes from needing to be settled in public. This is potentially both highly expensive and very damaging to the reputation of the organization. Policy should address clear messages to the legal authorities to the effect that the service sets out to be ethical, equitable and legally correct.

Fellow professionals

Finally, policy documentation should also send messages to the relevant professional communities. These should be messages of professional solidarity, supporting the initiatives of professional associations as expressed in their codes of conduct. The policy should seek to be a model that other organizations can emulate and something that is capable of being cited to good effect in public debate. It should be capable of giving encouragement to the individual working in situations where day-to-day contact with professional colleagues is infrequent and where an institutional policy has not been put in place. Good policy can set an example that has a much wider resonance than just within the organization for which it was framed.

What makes a good policy?

The characteristics of a good policy depend to some extent on precisely what you are aiming to achieve, but any good policy should have certain general features.

- Strength. The message should be wholeheartedly delivered and give every impression of being confidently believed. The tone of the document needs to be firm and assertive, but it is not just a matter of tone. The content itself needs to suggest that it is based on strong principles to which there is a complete commitment. If the documents communicate compromise and uneven commitment then their effect will instantly be diluted.

- Coherence. The strength of the message will be much greater if what is set out can all be seen to be part of a complete concept in which the various parts all complement and support each other. Care needs to be taken both to achieve this consistency and to bring it out in the documents.
- Clarity. The language of the documents needs to be clear, simple (in the best sense of the word) and free from ambiguity. The documents need to be clear to be persuasive. Not everyone in each of the stakeholder groups is likely to agree with every word, but if the case is good and the reader can understand it, there is a better chance that they will accept it. Officialese and legalese should be avoided in favour of plain everyday language. Clarity will help to avoid disputes and to resolve them when they do occur.
- Responsiveness. The documents should show that the policy is a principled response to concerns and that it respects the ideas of the community to be served. Policy ought ideally to be for all time, but things change and the policy ought not to seem to close the doors to this. The way to ensure that policy can be shown to incorporate response to change in circumstances and public perceptions is by building in a feedback and review mechanism. A policy will then have a capacity for renewing itself and maintaining its level of relevance.

So how do you create something that meets these requirements? The main answer to that question, and one that everyone can follow, is by carrying out a thorough process of preparation and delivery.

The process

Preparing good policy will take time, but how much time is a matter of the urgency involved and the human resources that can be committed to the job. A list of 12 elements that should form part of the process follows.

The list may seem very long and suggest a degree of elaboration that will be impossible under most circumstances. It is true that in practice the amount of time and effort that circumstances allow to be devoted to each element is going to vary a great deal. However, it is advisable, despite the general potential urgency and need to have documents available for use as soon as possible, that none of these elements be completely neglected. A really good policy cannot be delivered overnight and a process that is slimmed down too far may well lead to a policy that is deficient in some vital aspect.

1 **Research.** There is an enormous amount of policy-related documentation in both print and electronic form that ought to be scanned as a preliminary to policy making. Some of this will probably have formed part of the current awareness of any information professional, but other material, for instance that from professional areas such as computer systems, business or law, will need to be sought out specially.
2 **Consultation.** A thorough consultative process is needed both to gather relevant knowledge and obtain opinions from stakeholders (including the information professionals who will administer policy), and also to draw on the expertise of specialists in areas such as the law and computer systems.
3 **Brainstorming.** A wide input of policy ideas from members of the organization, whatever their status, length of service and qualifications, is an appropriate way of turning the consultative process towards the actual making of policy. This will involve short meetings and encouragement of contributors to put forward ideas independently of meetings.
4 **Drafting.** The material collected from stages 1–3 should then be used to create policy drafts. This can be the work of a designated individual, or a small group of three or four members working in very close association. They should sketch out the shape of documents and suggest forms of words to deal with the various topics to be covered.
5 **Internal circulation and redrafting.** Drafts should then be circulated, preferably widely, discussed in meetings called for that purpose, and both content and wording thoroughly debated. The documents should then be redrafted, as many times as seems necessary so as to come up with a version in which everyone feels confident.
6 **External scrutiny.** Agreed drafts then need to be looked at for accuracy and acceptability by the members of the same stakeholder and expert groups that were consulted at an earlier stage. This is a delicate stage because some of the decisions taken in the drafting process could easily open the whole matter up to fresh debate. The basic content of the policy is now, however, the responsibility of the organization and it ought to be confident enough to look only for comments on points of detail.
7 **Formal acceptance.** The policy documentation must be presented to the organization's controlling body for formal approval. Because the members

of this body should have also been informed and consulted throughout the process, this ought to be more or less a formality. Some final changes and adjustments should nevertheless be anticipated at this stage.

8 **Preparation for implementation**. Staff should be aware of the content of the policy as a result of their involvement in the process of creating it. However, they will still need training in the routines of administering it. They will need to know what to tell new users, what help they can be expected to give to users, how and when they should intervene unasked, and how precisely to deal with disputes and difficulties. They will have the day-to-day responsibility for delivering access with assurance and they must be properly prepared for this.

9 **Delivery of policy**. The AUP that will form part of the policy documentation has to be drawn to the attention of new users and it has to be conveniently available so that established users are in a position to remind themselves of its content. There are three obvious ways that this can be done: distributing it as a handout, displaying it as a poster, and showing it on the institution's website. Electronic delivery is much the most practical of the three because it associates the policy with the activity of using the system. However, one or both of the others can reinforce its effect.

10 **Review of (disciplinary) actions**. There is a strong case for saying that every occasion on which staff have to intervene to resolve difficulties between users or prevent use that is considered unacceptable should be recorded. This is both for future reference and to allow review of the occurrence of cases. This may seem much too burdensome a procedure, but since intervention ought to be practised as infrequently as possible recording can be kept at a minimum. Certainly any intervention that involves a user's privileges being temporarily or permanently suspended must be recorded. Cases of this kind ought then to be reviewed by the manager immediately responsible, to assess whether the decision was appropriate and to look for implications for the service's policy.

11 **Policy review**. At regular intervals – annually would seem like a sensible period – a policy review ought to be carried out. This can use the records of administration of the service, particularly the disciplinary records resulting from 10. It can also take account of other aspects, including the development of the internet, changes resulting from new hardware and software, new service priorities, and staffing changes. The process ought

also to be open to feedback from users and other stakeholders.

12 **Policy revision**. The review process will inevitably suggest the need for revisions in policy, preferably minor adjustments but possibly substantial shifts. Revision of policy closes the feedback loop and offers a response to the experience of administering the service, and to changes in circumstances.

Research

The research that you need to do for practical purposes is quite different from academic research. It very definitely does not have to be comprehensive in the way that a literature review for a dissertation may need to be. The important thing is to identify documents that give you the answers that you need, rather than to try to convince a reader that you have not missed anything that might just possibly be relevant. In this section I will say a little bit about the various types of material that may be useful to you, drawing your attention to some typical examples rather than setting out to identify everything that is likely to be useful. The bibliography and list of websites will refer you to other useful material, but they also do not set out to be comprehensive. This is a fast-moving field and there is no substitute for your own searches and current awareness scanning.

The literature

There are not many books dealing with policy for internet public access, although acceptable use policies are touched on briefly in many books about providing internet access in different types of institution, and there are some articles and websites. The exception is Smith (1999) *Internet policy handbook for libraries*, an American book that mainly covers similar ground to the present chapter, but does it rather differently. There is also a certain amount of published material on how to create policies in article form, for instance Campbell (1998).

Material with relevant approaches to ethics and law is reasonably common – for instance, books by Forester and Morrison (1994), Kling (1996) and Kallman and Grillo (1996), and articles in a broad spread of journals. There are also one or two specialist journals, *Journal of Information Ethics* (1992–) and *Ethics and Information Technology* (1999–) for example, and a reader by Stichler and Hauptman (1998).

Newspaper and magazine comment and debate are indispensable, though much of it is fairly fleeting: extremely interesting at the time, but swiftly superseded by new contributions. One of the best ways of keeping up to date with a topic that appears under various headings in the news (information technology, law, education and child welfare, to mention only a few obvious ones) is to scan a quality newspaper regularly. To pull together references from past years you can use the online versions that provide a searchable alternative to back copies of the printed version.

Professional journals contain similar news stories, but also debate and analysis that is usually more relevant and often more substantial than the average news item. For instance, *American Libraries* and the *Library Association Record* have regularly included helpful items for several years now. Indexing and abstracting services, such as *Library and Information Science Abstracts* or *Library Literature*, are an effective source of references to relevant items from the professional literature. There is also a good deal of material from organizations such as NCH Action for Children, their *Children on the internet: opportunities and hazards*, for example (Carr and Mullins, 1998).

Academic and research literature is capable of being helpful, but there is not a great deal of material in this category that is likely to be significant for your purposes. Law journals do contain some long and densely referenced treatments of relevant topics, and the information systems and technology literature has articles discussing internet control software and management systems from a technical point of view. Research literature specifically concerned with public internet access services is not all that common yet, but examples such as Turner and Kendall (2000) and Willson and Oulton (2000) show the sort of investigations that have been carried out.

The laws and official publications are an important resource, but the published texts of the law are not intended to be read by the general public (despite the dictum that 'Ignorance of the law is no defence'). Fortunately, there are plenty of good books and articles explaining and commenting on the law: Armstrong (1999), Jones (1996), Lloyd (1993), Marett (1991) and Smith (1996), to name only a selection.

Other people's policy documentation is perhaps the most obvious resource when drawing up your own policy. Copies of policy documents can usually be obtained just by asking, but this is a time-consuming exercise if a representative collection is sought. Published collections of policies exist and they provide a useful short cut. There is an American collection put together by the National Association of Regional Media Centers (1996), for example.

Internet content

As you would expect for a topic concerning the internet, the internet itself is a particularly fruitful source indeed of relevant material. Putting terms like 'Acceptable Use Policies' or 'Filtering' into a search engine produces as many examples and related documents as you could wish. A large percentage of the published documentation mentioned above is also available via the WWW. The most important internet resources tend to fall into three categories: the websites of campaigning bodies and of commercial organizations; discussion groups and listservs; and the sites of other institutions providing internet public access.

- Pressure group sites are very evident in this area, Electronic Frontier Foundation, Global Internet Liberties Campaign, Center for Democracy and Technology, and many others. There are organizations specifically set up to give ethical leadership, or to act as forums for ethical debate such as IFLA's FAIFE. There are also the commercial sites that promote filtering products, such as that of SurfControl. All of these and others are included in the List of Selected Websites, but there are always many more to be found via search engines and links within sites. Websites with guidance on how to draw up policies are also plentiful, for instance ASSET (2001) and Kent County Council (2000).
- Discussion groups and listservs on all types of ethical area (bioethics, business ethics, legal ethics, environmental research, etc.) are extremely plentiful and they include many with a direct relevance to this area. For instance, Unesco's VF-INFOethics (2001), the Ethics in Computing (2001) listserv, and the website Center for Professional and Applied Ethics (2001) at Valdosta University, which has many links. The International Center for Information Ethics (ICIE, 2001) is particularly helpful, but there are so many that the best way to find one to suit your needs, with a current URL, is to use a search engine.
- Sites of institutions providing public access to the internet are again too numerous to mention. A good starting place is the UNESCO Libraries Portal (2001). To see what a specific portal facility looks like you could try

the internet Public Library (2001), provided by the School of Information at the University of Michigan. Existing portals and gateways are many, and easy to trace by the usual methods. Tracing laws online is becoming easier all the time and discussions of law portals in Whittle (2001) and Greenleaf (2001) show how this works.

Consultation

Stakeholders

The research process described above can provide some information about stakeholder interests and opinions, but a consultation process related directly to the institution's own community is vital. If nothing else it is important as a way of building a sense that the resulting policy is owned by the community and not just by the information professionals, who will of course have been included in the consultation process.

- **Users**. To assess the opinions of users and potential users, there is a good case for a survey. The value of a survey is that its results offer a systematic view of who does, or will, use the service, what they want from a service and maybe why they want it, their preferences and other opinions. If a survey is impractical, putting out a call for people to send in their views and to attend consultative meetings will have to suffice. Of course, any organizations of users, such as library clubs or friends of the museum, must be invited to take part in the process. These forms of consultation do identify opinion, but it is important to remember that it is likely to be the opinion of those already committed to one view or another. The background opinions of the uncommitted may well be lost in this form of consultation.
- **Staff**. Some of the most expert people available for consultation will be on the staff of the organization. They will certainly be the best informed about local circumstances. Not to consult them would be wasteful of this expertise. It is also true that policies of which staff do not feel ownership are almost guaranteed to be ineffective policies: they will be ignored as far as possible, and even subverted when the opportunity occurs. Consultation of staff, and making policy that takes account of what the consultation produces, are as important as the final content of the policy documentation itself. It does not mean that policy is the sum of what the

staff want. It means that by the time policy is documented in forms designed to be used and administered by staff a process of discussion and persuasion will have been fully worked through.

- **Community groups**. Alongside consultation of users it is important to obtain the opinion of representatives of specific groups that may feel themselves affected, or that will have special needs of some kind. Included in the list of the groups that might be included in the consultation process are (in no particular order of significance) religious congregations, schools and colleges, parents' groups, students' unions, ethnic and linguistic minorities, people with disabilities, clubs and societies, local business and industry, and trades unions.
- **Funders, elected councils, management committees, regulators**. It almost goes without saying that the views of responsible bodies must be obtained at an early stage of the process. Unless their requirements are satisfied the whole exercise may turn out to be a waste of effort, so it pays to find out what they feel about providing public internet access.

Experts

In addition to consulting those who have a stake in the service, it is important not to forget what those with special expertise and experience can contribute. Your research should have identified publications and websites containing expert opinion, but clarification and advice on things peculiar to your own institution may well be needed. The kinds of people who might be consulted include some or all of the following.

- **Legal advisers**. The broad legal position can easily be obtained from various sources, but it would be foolish not to consult professional lawyers over anything that gives serious cause for doubt. Of course this will cost money, but it will be a necessary expense that might save money in the future.
- **Professional associations**. It is a core function of professional associations to provide advice and guidance to their members and to the general public through the documentation that they create, and in direct response to enquiries. These are services that you should take advantage of, because as members of a professional association you have paid for them. They have the great virtue of providing guidance rooted in a professional viewpoint that you share.

- **Relevant NGOs.** Non-governmental organizations dealing with an enormous range of relevant subjects, such as freedom of information, internet issues, consumer affairs, child protection, and education, exist in great numbers. They generally welcome approaches for advice and guidance.

- **Software and systems experts.** The setting up of a system to serve members of the public who want to use the internet brings with it a whole series of questions to which technical answers will be needed. You have to consult technical experts, whether they are outside consultants, computer services people from within the organization, or representatives of software and systems companies. The important thing is to get answers to the questions you want to ask, not the questions that they think that you should ask. With this proviso, their advice is indispensable.

- **Experienced colleagues.** There is invariably someone else who has been through an experience similar to the one that you will have when creating your own policy. They are generally eager to discuss this and pass on the fruits of their experience. The virtue of what they will tell you is that it is practical and tested in the real world, as opposed to discussed in the committee room.

The acceptable use policy

Each of the 12 stages in policy making, outlined earlier, applies to your general policy on internet access and its documentation. But the public delivery of that policy, in the form of what is usually called an acceptable use policy, is crucial. Before saying more about the AUP, I must point out that I have something of a problem with the word 'acceptable' in this, because it leads to the question 'Acceptable to whom?'. Almost any answer to this question raises the further question 'What right has whoever it is to decide what is acceptable or unacceptable?'. For this reason I prefer a more neutral term such as 'internet use policies'. However, I recognize that I would be confusing the issue if I insisted on a term that people were not familiar with, and that did not instantly convey the same sense of its significance that a familiar term does. So I will follow normal practice and call it the acceptable use policy.

Almost all institutions that are offering public internet access have an AUP in a form that they can present to the public. These existing AUPs vary from the comprehensive to the rudimentary and in plenty of cases they say as little as possible. Lack of detail may be quite a good thing while things go smoothly (the 'Least said, soonest mended' principle). A very short, direct document has the enormous virtue that it definitely increases the chance that people will remember what it says. When problems occur, however, it becomes necessary to go back to internal documentation and work out what the public policy documents should have said. This is difficult to do when under pressure. It is to some extent futile because it is difficult to take into account things that were not actually set out formally to the public. It is also frustrating because an incident might never have occurred in the first place if there had been an explicit policy statement available. A balance needs to be struck between keeping the AUP simple and making sure that truly essential information is included.

Models for the AUP

If we look for models, we find that acceptable use has probably been worked out most thoroughly in the academic sector. The JANET acceptable use policy (JANET, 2001) contains clear statements on the whole range of issues that might arise from internet use and offers penalties for those who disregard the policy. The interesting thing is that a specific institution may well feel that it is necessary to create something even more thorough and explicit (see Appendix 4). Of course an academic institution's acceptable use policy is not quite the same thing as a policy for public access points provided by an information institution such as a library. The academic policy covers a number of issues that are only likely to arise when it is members of the institution (staff and students) using the facilities essentially for the purposes of their work and their studies. Other types of use (personal e-mail, and recreational use of the WWW, Usenet newsgroups, etc.) are explicitly withdrawable privileges, not rights.

On the other hand, use for purely personal purposes is the whole purpose of true public access points. A policy for a general public access point can quite reasonably be much more to the point, precisely because there is no need to distinguish between use for institutional or personal purposes. The AUP needs to be a distillation of the practical implications of policy, addressed to a general readership in the clearest possible language. A good AUP will be short, direct and relevant. The examples in the appendices are reasonably typical, but it is possible to scan great numbers, either on organizations' own websites, or in collections helpfully put together for just this purpose. Some try to cover all of the main possibilities for dispute, but others contain only the barest and most essential of statements.

Looking at examples of documentation from other institutions is definitely helpful. No doubt there are plenty of organizations that have created their own documentation by mimicking an existing AUP discovered in this way, or cobbling together pieces from several. This may function reasonably effectively, but is not an especially good way of obtaining an AUP for two reasons. First, if you believe that your organization has unique features, it is unlikely that by 'borrowing' your AUP content you will truly obtain something that fits its own particular needs. Secondly, following a thorough process of preparation, as outlined in this chapter, will mean that a policy that you create yourselves will be owned by everyone connected with the organization in a way that no borrowed policy could ever be. That said, there are essential features to an AUP.

Essential features

You will find that opinions on the essential features of the AUP do differ and will appear in slightly varying ways in the guides to making an AUP that are on offer (see Appendix 2). I have summed them up here under seven headings.

1 **Aims and objectives.** The AUP needs to begin with an explanation of why the service is provided and what it seeks to achieve. This will vary greatly between libraries of different kinds, information centres, schools and colleges, museums and archives. Getting it clear why the service is there, whether it is intended for all kinds of information seeking, includes recreational use (or not), or is only to support certain kinds of study, is vital in allowing the user to make sense of the other sections of the AUP.

2 **Eligibility.** It needs to be stated whether the service is available to all, or members of the organization only, whether it is necessary to register as a user, whether the service is for children and young people as well as adults, or if it is a service specifically for children and young people. If young people need formal permission from a parent to use the service or if they need to be accompanied by an adult this also needs to be made clear.

3 **Scope**. The boundaries and limits of the service need to be set out. This is particularly important in a closed community such as a college or a business firm. Here it will usually be stated whether or not use for personal purposes (which is what makes the service to a limited extent a public facility) is allowed or not. The possibility of certain limited kinds of non-essential use, such as study for professional qualifications, or work for a trade union, might be mentioned as exceptions to a general ban on personal use. Also in truly public service institutions it has to be made clear whether access is full or limited in some way. For instance, limitations might be WWW only with no e-mail or chat facilities. Most significant of all, it needs to be stated whether the service is filtered or not, and if so to what extent. If printing and downloading are not allowed, that needs to be stated. It also needs to be clear if payment will be required or not, and if so, for what aspects of the service.

4 **Illegal use**. It ought not to be necessary to mention illegal use, but it definitely is. A blanket reminder that illegal use is forbidden is not a great deal of use without drawing the user's attention to the main areas this covers. Infringement of intellectual property rights, defamation, hacking, spreading of viruses, and infringement of privacy and data protection law might be mentioned specifically.

5 **Unacceptable use**. This is more contentious because it is harder to define. Some services forbid access to material that is not illegal, but is seen as unacceptable: sexual content, particularly for young users, is what this generally means. Courtesy towards other users, avoidance of disruption, and in particular avoidance of anything that might be construed as harassment, could also be stressed.

6 **Service commitments**. A statement of what levels of service the organization seeks to provide may be included and it can be linked to disclaimers, such as warning that the accuracy and legality of material from the WWW cannot be guaranteed in any way. A reference to the organization's own privacy policy may be included under this heading. The way in which challenges to the services will be handled can be specified at this point.

7 **User commitments**. The user may be asked to sign up to the policy in a formal way and by doing so signify acceptance of a disciplinary procedure, including the possibility of suspension of the right to use the service. The way in which this will be handled and the means of appealing against decisions will then need to be set out.

Final checklist

To conclude, once you have developed a policy for public access to the internet, you should be able to look at both your internal documentation and your AUP, and give positive answers to some broad general questions. These form a kind of final checklist to complete the policy-making process.

Ethical, legal and practical?

* The first part of this question is the hardest to answer: one person's ethical policy can be someone else's crime against humanity. All that you can hope to achieve is something that you and colleagues can live with and still retain a clear conscience. It ought to be possible to argue through the policy in terms of some coherent ethical approach and justify what the policy implies in those same terms. The specific test of whether the ethical approach works for the information professional is whether it is conducive to the protection and enhancement of freedom of expression and freedom of access to information.
* Conformity with the law is mainly a matter of getting the detail right. Certainly no professional should risk misinforming people about their legal position in relation to a service that is being provided. Nor can a professional openly defy the law in publicly available policy statements. This is a real difficulty on those occasions (not so infrequent) when the law is obviously out of kilter with the times, or when it is obscure and more or less impossible to apply. There are also the problems that the principled professional experiences in countries where the laws and their enforcement are obviously unjust. Most of the time, however, it is a matter of saying enough to draw attention to the laws that apply and leaving the complications till later.
* Practicality is a crucial test of the policy. Expressing high principles that cannot be delivered in practice is merely a way of creating a little temporary happiness through words. The problem with practicality as a test is that it can be a route to damaging compromise and the dilution of essential principles. The temptation to say that policy must simply be a version of what you can afford, or what people will accept, will always be there. Practicality cannot be the only test, nor should it be the first, but it is a test that must be passed.

Responsive to public concern?

Three major issues against which policy should test well are human dignity, intellectual property, and privacy.

- Human dignity is the most testing of all. For many people the presence of pornography and other distasteful material on the internet makes it a contaminated medium, particularly for children's use. A policy needs to provide assurance that the service is safe to use, without compromising freedom of information principles. How the question of filtering and blocking is handled is central to this.
- The issue of intellectual property on the internet is fundamentally contentious because of the way in which electronic recording and communication of information questions the principles on which the law has been based. Holders of intellectual property rights need to feel assured that a policy reinforces protection of their material when it is used at public access points, and internet users need clear guidance as to what is permissible.
- Privacy is a source of growing public concern because of fears about the security of internet business transactions, official monitoring of communications, and the mischievous or malicious activities of hackers, crackers and the spreaders of viruses. The policy needs to assure users that they will be as safe as possible from this type of hazard when using public access points. It also needs to demonstrate that the institution itself is not monitoring internet use in ways that could be to the detriment of users.

In the best interests of stakeholders?

The term 'best interests' signifies that this involves a professional judgement of what is needed for the crucial stakeholder groups: users, staff and the responsible authorities.

- The best interests of a group as diverse as users of a public internet access service are not easy to sum up, but a serious attempt must be made to do this so that the policy can be assessed. Probably the best principle to apply is respect for the autonomy of users as individuals. Does the policy allow them to operate as responsible people, pursuing their own paths of discovery in a way constrained only by the law and basic consideration for others?

- Staff need a policy that they can implement confidently and effectively. They must be able to believe in it, or at least believe that as a team they will unite in working to maintain it. They must feel that it protects both them and the more vulnerable of the users. For them, the test of practicality will matter a great deal.
- Funders, councils, committees and regulators have the legal responsibility for the service and this carries with it the whole body of ethical and practical concerns. They must be assured not only that the service provides value for money and makes a contribution to society, but that it is acceptable to the general public, for whom they stand as representatives. Public opinion, as reflected by the votes in elections and commentary in the media, is a vital test for them. Therefore to satisfy them the policy must satisfy the public as a whole.

A personal wish

Throughout this book I have tried to argue that every institution providing public internet access needs good policy, but as far as I am able, I have tried to avoid telling you exactly what that policy should be. This is a book about how to make policy, not a set of policy recommendations. It will no doubt be fairly obvious what my own position is on the major issues and I was fortunate to have the opportunity to develop my own views in drawing up a set of policy guidelines for the Council of Europe (see Appendix 5). These were explicitly intended to assert the values of freedom of expression and freedom of access to information. These are values to which the Council of Europe is very strongly committed, and the Council's Cultural Policy advisers felt that there was a danger that they would get lost in the sound and fury over internet content. The guidelines went through a lengthy process of discussion and re-drafting, including a major consultative conference in Helsinki in 1999, and two full meetings of the Culture Committee. The resulting document has had the critical attention of information professionals and representatives of almost all European governments (including a jovial Monsignor from the Vatican). My personal wish is that you will find the guidelines useful in the process of policy making and that you will succeed in producing policy that both meets your needs and stays true to the basic principles that the guidelines uphold.

References

Armstrong, C. J. (ed.) (1999) *Staying legal: a guide to issues and practice for users and publishers of electronic resources*, London, Library Association Publishing.

ASSET (2001) *Creating an acceptable use policy for a school online system*, available at
www.asset.asu.edu/accepuse.htm

Campbell, S. (1998) Guidelines for writing children's internet policies, *American Libraries*, **29** (1), 91–2.

Carr, J. and Mullins, A. (1998). *Children on the internet: opportunities and hazards*, London, NCH Action for Children.

Center for Professional and Applied Ethics, Valdosta University (2001)
http://valdosts.edu/cpae

Ethics and Information Technology (1999–) Dordrecht, Netherlands, Kluwer.

Ethics in Computing (2001) **Ethics-l@listserv.gmd.de**

Forester, T. and Morrison, P. (1994) *Computer ethics: cautionary tales and ethical dilemmas in computing*, 2nd edn, Cambridge, Mass, MIT Press.

Greenleaf, G. (2001) Solving the problems of finding law on the web: World Law and DIAL, *International Journal of Legal Information*, **29** (2), 383–419.

ICIE (International Center for Information Ethics) (2001)
http://icie.zkm.de

IFLA/FAIFE (2001)
www.faife.dk

Internet Public Library, University of Michigan (2001)
www.ipl.org

JANET (2001) *Acceptable use policy*, available at
www.ja.net/documents/use.html

Jones, H. (1996) *Publishing law*, London, Routledge.

Journal of Information Ethics (1992–) Jefferson, NC, McFarland and Co.

Kallman, E. and Grillo, J. (1996) *Ethical decision making and information technology*, 2nd edn, New York, McGraw Hill.

Kent County Council (2000) *Internet access policy 2000: a template for schools*, available at
www.kented.org.uk/ngfl/policy.html

Kling, R. (ed.) (1996) *Computerization and controversy: value conflicts and social choices*, 2nd edn, San Diego, Academic Press.

Lloyd, I. (1993) *Information technology law*, London, Butterworths.

Marett, P. (1991) *Information law and practice*, Aldershot, Gower.

National Association of Regional Media Centers (1996) *Anthology of internet acceptable use policies*, Sioux Center, Iowa, National Association of Regional Media Centers.

Smith, G. (ed.) (1996) *Internet law and regulation: a specially commissioned report*, London, FT Law and Tax.

Smith, M. (1999) *Internet policy handbook for libraries*, New York, Neal-Schuman.

Stichler, R. and Hauptman, R. (eds) (1998) *Ethics, information and technology: readings*, Jefferson, NC, McFarland and Co.

Turner, K. and Kendall, M. (2000) Public use of the Internet at Chester Library, *Information Research*, 5 (3).

UNESCO Libraries Portal (2001)
www.unesco.org/webworld/portal-bib/library-websites

UNESCO VF-INFOethics (2001)
www.unesco.org/webworld/infoethics

Whittle, S. (2001) Finding law in the twenty first century: an introduction to the SOSIG Law Gateway, *International Journal of Legal Information*, 29 (2), 360–82.

Willson, J. and Oulton, T. (2000) Controlling access to the internet in UK public libraries, *OCLC Systems and Services*, 16 (4), 194–201.

Reading list

A list of published material for reading around the topic of the book, selected from the items cited in the chapters, but also including some additional material.

Background

Alderman, J. (2001) *Sonic boom: Napster, P2P and the battle for the future of music*, London, Fourth Estate.

Bangemann, M. (1994) *Europe and the global information society: recommendations to the European Council*, Luxembourg, European Commission.

Capitanchik, D. and Whine, M. (1996) *The governance of cyberspace: racism on the internet*, London, Institute for Jewish Policy Research.

Carr, J. and Mullins, A. (1998). *Children on the internet: opportunities and hazards*, London, NCH Action for Children.

Cronin, B. and Davenport, E. (2001) E–Rogenous zones: positioning pornography in the digital economy, *Information Society*, **17** (1), 33–48.

Diamond, E. and Bates, S. (1995) Law and order comes to cyberspace, *MIT Technology Review*, **98** (October), 22–33.

Lewis, M. (2001) *The future just happened*, London, Hodder.

McMurdo, G. (1997) Cyberporn and communication decency, *Journal of Information Science*, **23** (1), 81–90.

Resnick, P. and Miller, J. (1996) PICS: internet access controls without censorship, *Communications of the ACM*, **39** (10), 87–93.

Resnick, P. and Varian, H. R. (eds) (1997) Recommender systems, special section of *Communications of the ACM*, **40** (3), 56–89.

Shrybman, S. (2000) Information, commodification and the World Trade Organisation, *IFLA Journal*, **26** (5–6), 354–61.

Wallace, J. and Mangan, M. (1996) *Sex, laws and cyberspace*, New York, Henry Holt and Co.

Ethics and law

Armstrong, C. J. (ed.) (1999) *Staying legal: a guide to issues and practice for users and publishers of electronic resources*, London, Library Association Publishing.

Cavazos, E. A. and Morin, G. (1994) *Cyberspace and the law*, Cambridge, Mass, MIT Press.

Eisenschitz, T. (1998) Internet law and information policy, *Aslib Proceedings*, **50** (9), 267–73.

Faucette, J.E. (1995) The freedom of speech at risk in cyberspace, *Duke Law Journal*, **44** (6), 1155–82.

Forester, T. and Morrison, P. (1994) *Computer ethics: cautionary tales and ethical dilemmas in computing*, 2nd edn, Cambridge, Mass, MIT Press.

Foskett, D. (1962) *The creed of the librarian – no politics, no religion, no morals*, London, Library Association.

Greenleaf, G. (2001) Solving the problem of finding law on the web: World Law and DIAL, *International Journal of Legal Information*, **29** (2), 383–419.

Hauptman, R. (1976) Professionalism or culpability? An experiment in ethics, *Wilson Library Bulletin*, **50** (8), 626–7.

Hill, M.(1997) Facing up to dilemmas: conflicting ethics and the modern information professional, *FID News Bulletin*, **47** (4), 107–17.

Jones, H. (1996) *Publishing law*, London, Routledge.

Juznic, P. et al. (2001) Excuse me, how do I commit suicide? Access to ethically debatable items of information in public libraries, *Library Management*, **22** (2), 75–9.

Kallman, E. and Grillo, J. (1996) *Ethical decision making and information technology*, 2nd edn, New York, McGraw Hill.

Kanter, R. (2000) Legal issues resulting from internet use in public libraries, *Feliciter*, **46** (1), 18–19.

Kling, R. (ed.) (1996) *Computerization and controversy: value conflicts and social choices*, 2nd edn, San Diego, Academic Press.

Koren, M. (1996) *Tell me! The right of the child to information*, The Hague, NBLC.

Lloyd, I. (1993) *Information technology law*, London, Butterworths.

Marett, P. (1991) *Information law and practice*, Aldershot, Gower.

Nelson, N. (2001) Legal and liability issues related to internet access, *Library Administration and Management*, **15** (1), 14–16.

Palfrey, T. (1997) Pornography and the possible criminal liability of internet service providers under the Obscene Publications and Protection of Children Acts, *Information and Communications Technology Law*, **6** (3), 187–99.

Shea, V. (1994). *Netiquette*, San Francisco, Albion Books.

Sherwill–Navarro, P. (1998) Internet in the workplace: censorship, liability and freedom of speech, *Medical Reference Services Quarterly*, **17** (4), 77–84.

Smith, G. (ed.) (1996) *Internet law and regulation: a specially commissioned report*, London, FT Law and Tax.

Stichler, R. and Hauptman, R. (eds) (1998) *Ethics, information and technology: readings*, Jefferson, NC, McFarland and Co.

Sturges, P. (2001) The library and freedom of information: agent or icon? *Alexandria*, **13** (1), 3–16.

Sturges, P., Teng, V. and Iliffe, U. (2001) User privacy in the digital library environment: a matter of concern for information professionals, *Library Management*, **22** (8/9), 364–70.

Vitiello, G. (1997) Information on the internet – limits to freedom of expression? *Focus*, **28** (3), 130–42.

Wengert, R. (2001) Some ethical aspects of being an information professional, *Library Trends*, **49** (3), 486–509.

Whittle, S. (2001) Finding law in the twenty first century: an introduction to the SOSIG Law Gateway, *International Journal of Legal Information*, **29** (2), 360–82.

Management and policy

Albitz, R. S. (2001) Establishing access policies for emerging media in academic libraries: the video lending experience as a model, *Collection Management*, **25** (3), 1–9.

Balas, J. L. (1998) Debating public access to the internet, *Computers in Libraries*, **18** (3), 42–4.

Betcher, A. (2000) Strikeout or home run? Managing public access to the internet, *Computers in Libraries*, **20** (4), 28–33.

Branch, B. and Conable, G. (1997) To filter or not to filter, *American Libraries*, **28** (6), 100–2.

Bruce, C. (1997) *Seven faces of information literacy*, Adelaide, Auslib Press.

Burt, D. (1997) In defense of filtering, *American Libraries*, **28** (7), 46–8.

Campbell, S. (1998) Guidelines for writing children's internet policies, *American Libraries*, **29** (1), 91–2.

Estabrook, L. (1996) Sacred trust or competitive opportunity: using patron records, *Library Journal*, **121** (2), 48–9.

Estabrook, L. and Lakner, E. (2000) Managing internet access: results of a national survey, *American Libraries*, **31** (8), 60–2.

Grafstein, A.J. (1999) The public library and the internet: who has the right to what? *Internet Reference Services Quarterly*, **4** (2), 7–19.

Harper, S., Newton, R. and Dixon, D. (1999) Instant access: or filter? *Public Library Journal*, **14** (2), 46–7.

Hyman, K. (1997) Internet policies: managing in the real world, *American Libraries*, **28** (11), 60–3.

Janssen, A. (2000) Freedom of speech, sexual harassment and internet filters in academic libraries, *Journal of Information Ethics*, **9** (2), 37–45.

Kiribige, H. M. (2001) Internet access in public libraries: results of an end user targeted pilot study 1997–2000, *Information Technology and Libraries*, **20** (2), 113–15.

Konomos, P. and Herrington, S. (2000) Evaluating the use of public PC workstations at the Arizona State University libraries, *Electronic Library*, **18** (6), 403–6.

Krug, J. F. (2000) Internet and filtering in libraries: the American experience, *IFLA Journal*, **26** (4), 284–7.

Liff, S., Steward, F. and Watts, P. (1999) Public access to the internet: new approaches from internet cafés and community technology centres, *New Review of Information Networking*, **5**, 27–41.

Mason, M. G. (1997) Sex, kids and the public library, *American Libraries*, **28** (6), 104–6.

National Association of Regional Media Centers (1996) *Anthology of internet acceptable use policies*, Sioux Center, Iowa, National Association of Regional Media Centers.

Nicefaro, M. E. (1998) Internet use policies, *Online*, **22** (5), 31–3.

Schneider, K. (1997) *A practical guide to internet filters*, New York, Neal-Schuman.

Shim, J., Qureshi, A. and Siegel, J. (2000) *The international handbook of computer security*, Chicago, Glenlake.

Smith, M. (1999) *Internet policy handbook for libraries*, New York, Neal–Schuman.

Turner, K. and Kendall, M. (2000) Public use of the internet at Chester Library, *Information Research*, **5** (3).

Webber, S. and Johnston, B. (2000) Information literacy: new perspectives and implications, *Journal of Information Science*, **26** (6), 381–97.

Weessies, K. and Wales, B. (1999) Internet policies in midsized academic libraries, *Reference and User Services Quarterly*, **39** (1), 33–41.

Willson J. and Oulton, T. (2000) Controlling access to the internet in UK public libraries, *OCLC Systems and Services*, **16** (4), 194–201.

Selected websites

Acceptable use policies: a handbook, available at
www.pen.k12va.us/go/VDOE/technology/AUP/home.shtml
Provides many resources for making policies. From Virginia Department of Education.

American Library Association
www.ala.org
The best site for documents on library-related aspects.

ARMA International (The Association of Records Managers and Administrators)
www.arma.org
Records management resources from the most prominent professional association in the field.

Bluehighways
www.bluehighways.com
Contains The Internet Filter Assessment Project (TIFAP) and other documents.

Censorship and Intellectual Freedom Page
http://php.indiana.edu/~quinnjf/censor.html
Provides links to many other relevant sites and Usenet groups.

Censorware and Filtering in Libraries
http://burn.ucsd.edu/~mai/library/index.html
Anti filtering site.

Censorware Project
www.censorware.net
Carries news and product analyses on filtering.

Center for Democracy and Technology
www.cdt.org
Advocates public policies advancing civil liberties in the networked environment.

CILIP: the Chartered Institute of Library and Information Professionals
   www.cilip.org.uk
   See Library Association
Computer & Information Ethics Resources on WWW
   www.ethics.ubc.ca/resources/computer.html
   Canadian site with many links.
Computer Professionals for Social Responsibility
   www.cpsr.org/
   Includes material on filtering privacy, etc.
Cyber-Rights & Cyber-Liberties (UK)
   www.cyber-rights.org
   Many links and documents.
Electronic Frontier Foundation
   www.eff.org
   Many links and extensive archives on the site of the major campaigning body since 1990.
Electronic Privacy Information Center
   http://epic.org
   Site has many basic legislative documents and other resources.
Family Friendly Libraries
   www.fflibraries.org
   Campaigns to change library attitudes (as represented by the ALA position).
Global Internet Liberties Campaign
   www.gilc.org
   International campaigning organization for human rights on the internet.
ICA (International Council on Archives)
   www.ica.org
   The key site for archive-related material.
ICIE (International Center for Information Ethics)
   http://icie.zkm.de
   Provides an easily accessible collection of relevant materials.
ICOM (International Council of Museums)
   www.icom.org
   Provides a great deal of museum-related material, including the Code of Professional Ethics.
ICRA (Internet Content Rating Association)
   www.rsac.org

Provides the facilities to rate sites for filtering purposes.

IFLA/FAIFE

www.faife.dk

IFLA's freedom of information site.

INCORE

www.incore.org

European organization working on self-regulation and rating. Has received major EC funding.

Internet Content Register

www.internet.org.uk

Works under the slogan 'Making the Internet safer' and promotes the Internet Code of Practice (ICOP).

Internet Public Library

www.ipl.org

A portal giving access to a wealth of library-related resources.

Internet Watch Foundation (IWF)

www.iwf.org.uk

UK industry self-regulatory body, that provides a hotline for the reporting of problem content, particularly child pornography.

Library Association

After merger with the Institute of Information Scientists in 2002 represents a much wider range of UK information professionals, under the name CILIP: the Chartered Institute of Library and Information Professionals.

See CILIP: the Chartered Institute of Library and Information Professionals

Library Watch

http://netwinds.com/library

An online magazine campaigning for the protection of children in libraries.

MIT SAFE

www.mit.edu/activities/safe/home.html

MIT student organization against censorship which links to sample newsgroups.

National Coalition Against Censorship

www.ncac.org

Carries a very substantial Internet Filters Report.

NCH Action for Children

www.nchafc.org.uk

Includes a parents' internet guide.

Peacefire

www.peacefire.org

Student group's site that includes reports on filters and unblocking programs.

PICS (the Platform for Internet Content Selection)

www.w3.org/PICS

The official site describing and promoting PICS.

Responsible Netizen

http://netizen.uoregon.edu

Sets out to help young people use the internet with confidence.

SurfControl

www.surfcontrol.com

The site of a major monitoring and filtering product company, included here as a product-related example.

TRUSTe

www.truste.org

Independent industry organization dealing with privacy issues.

UNESCO Libraries Portal

www.unesco.org/webworld/portal-bib/library-websites

A portal that gives access to great numbers of library websites, many of which carry internet policy material.

VF-INFOethics

www.unesco.org/webworld/infoethics

UNESCO's virtual forum on information ethics.

Wired News

www.wired.com

E-journal with many relevant articles.

Appendices

Appendix I
Codes of conduct

1.1 American Library Association, Code of Ethics
www.ala.org/alaorg/oif/ethics.html

As members of the American Library Association, we recognize the importance of codifying and making known to the profession and to the general public the ethical principles that guide the work of librarians, other professionals providing information services, library trustees and library staffs.

Ethical dilemmas occur when values are in conflict. The American Library Association Code of Ethics states the values to which we are committed, and embodies the ethical responsibilities of the profession in this changing information environment.

We significantly influence or control the selection, organization, preservation, and dissemination of information. In a political system grounded in an informed citizenry we are members of a profession explicitly committed to intellectual freedom and the freedom of access to information. We have a special obligation to ensure the free flow of information and ideas to present and future generations.

The principles of this Code are expressed in broad statements to guide ethical decision making. These statements provide a framework; they cannot and do not dictate conduct to cover particular situations.

I. We provide the highest level of service to all library users through appropriate and usefully organized resources; equitable service policies; equitable access; and accurate, unbiased, and courteous responses to all requests.

II. We uphold the principles of intellectual freedom and resist all efforts to censor library resources.

III. We protect each library user's right to privacy and confidentiality with respect to information sought or received and resources consulted, borrowed, acquired or transmitted.

IV. We recognize and respect intellectual property rights.

V. We treat co-workers and other colleagues with respect, fairness and good faith, and advocate conditions of employment that safeguard the rights and welfare of all employees of our institutions.

VI. We do not advance private interests at the expense of library users, colleagues, or our employing institutions.

VII. We distinguish between our personal convictions and professional duties and do not allow our personal beliefs to interfere with fair representation of the aims of our institutions or the provision of access to their information resources.

VIII. We strive for excellence in the profession by maintaining and enhancing our own knowledge and skills, by encouraging the professional development of co-workers, and by fostering the aspirations of potential members of the profession.

Adopted by the ALA Council
June 28, 1995

(Reproduced by permission of the American Library Association)

1.2 American Library Association, Library Bill of Rights
www.ala.org/work/freedom/lbr.html

The American Library Association affirms that all libraries are forums for information and ideas, and that the following basic policies should guide their services.

I. Books and other library resources should be provided for the interest, information, and enlightenment of all people of the community the library serves. Materials should not be excluded because of the origin, background, or views of those contributing to their creation.

II. Libraries should provide materials and information presenting all points of view on current and historical issues. Materials should not be proscribed or removed because of partisan or doctrinal disapproval.

III. Libraries should challenge censorship in the fulfillment of their responsibility to provide information and enlightenment.

IV. Libraries should cooperate with all persons and groups concerned with resisting abridgment of free expression and free access to ideas.

V. A person's right to use a library should not be denied or abridged because of origin, age, background, or views.

VI. Libraries which make exhibit spaces and meeting rooms available to the public they serve should make such facilities available on an equitable basis, regardless of the beliefs or affiliations of individuals or groups requesting their use.

Adopted June 18, 1948.
Amended February 2, 1961, and January 23, 1980, inclusion
of 'age' reaffirmed January 23, 1996, by the ALA Council.

(Reproduced by permission of the American Library Association)

1.3 Library Association, Code of Professional Conduct
www.la-hq.org.uk/directory/about/conduct.html

1   Members of the Association must conduct themselves in such a way that their conduct would not be reasonably regarded by their professional colleagues within the field of librarianship (including the provision of information services) as serious professional misconduct or as professional misconduct. It is by this overall test that the conduct will be judged.

2a   Members must comply with the Charter and Bye-laws of the Association and the provisions of this Code of Conduct;

 b   Members must not engage in conduct which may seriously prejudice the standing and reputation of the library profession or of The Library Association.

 c   Members must be competent in their professional activities including the requirement

(i) to keep abreast of developments in librarianship in those branches of professional practice in which qualifications and experience entitle them to engage;

(ii) in respect of those members of the Association responsible for supervising the training and duties of another librarian, to ensure that those whom they supervise are trained to carry out their duties in a competent manner.

 d   Members' primary duty when acting in the capacity of librarian is to their clients, i.e. the persons or groups of persons for whose requirements and use are intended the resources and services which the members are engaged to provide. In all professional considerations the interests of the clients within their prescribed or legitimate requirements take precedence over all other interests. It is recognized that the persons or groups of persons to whom this duty is owed will vary according to the nature of the employment which members undertake. In particular it is recognized that different considerations will apply where members are working at a place to which the public has right of access from those where they are working in an environment where the public is excluded or given only limited access.

 e   In places to which the public has right of access, save where the flow of information must be restricted by reason of confidentiality, members have an obligation to facilitate the flow of information and ideas and to protect and promote the rights of every individual to have free and equal access to sources of information without discrimination and within the limits of the law.

f   Members must fulfil to the best of their ability the contractual obligations owed to their employer. However circumstances may arise when the public interest or the reputation of the profession itself may be at variance with the narrower interests of an employer. If it is found to be impossible to reconcile such difference then public interest and the maintenance of professional standards must be the primary considerations.

g   Members should not knowingly promote material the prime purpose of which is to encourage discrimination on the grounds of race, colour, creed, gender or sexual orientation. It shall not be regarded as promoting such material to divulge it for the purpose of studying the subject of that discrimination.

h   (i) Members must not divulge or permit to be divulged any materials, information or administrative record (in manual or electronic form) which has been entrusted to them in confidence, to any third party nor use such information without the prior consent of the client for any purpose other than that for which it was first obtained. This duty to the client continues after the relationship of librarian and client ceases.
(ii) Members are absolved from the duty set out in sub-paragraph (i) above in so far as is required by law and in so far as it is necessary to answer accusations before the Disciplinary Committee.

i   Members' actions and decisions should be determined solely by their professional judgement and they should not profit from their position otherwise than by normal remuneration or fee for professional services.

j   Members must report the facts to the Secretary of The Library Association if convicted of any offence involving dishonesty or one which brings the profession into disrepute.

k   Members must:
(i) respond to any requirements from the Disciplinary Committee for comments or information on a complaint;
(ii) attend the committee proceedings when required to do so, with such representation as is provided for in the Bye-Laws;

(iii) attend upon a nominated person for the purpose of receiving guidance as to future conduct if required to do so.

3a   Failure to comply with the requirements set out in paragraph 2, including the requirements relating to competence may, if proved before the Disciplinary Committee be regarded by it as serious professional misconduct and, if so, shall render the member concerned liable to be expelled or suspended (either unconditionally or subject to conditions) to be ordered to repay or forego fees and expenses as appropriate, or to be reprimanded and/or to be ordered to pay the costs of the hearing.

b   Failure to comply with the requirements set out in paragraph 2, which, in the opinion of the Disciplinary Committee, falls short of serious professional misconduct may, if proved, render the member liable to be admonished or to be given appropriate guidance as to his or her future conduct.

c   The provisions of Bye-Laws 44–46 shall apply.

(Reproduced by permission of CILIP: the Chartered Institute
of Library and Information Professionals)

Note: The Library Association merged with the Institute of Information Scientists in April 2002 to become CILIP: the Chartered Institute of Library and Information Professionals. A new Code of Professional Conduct is under preparation: please check the CILIP website **www.cilip.org.uk** for progress.

1.4 ARMA International, Code of Professional Responsibility
www.arma.org/publications/ethics.cfm

Purposes of the Code

This code is intended to increase the awareness of ethical issues among information and records management practitioners and to guide them in reflection, decision making, and action in two broad areas of ethical concern: society and the profession.

I: The Social Principles

Because of their responsibilities to society, information and records managers:

1. Support the free flow and oppose censorship of publicly available information as a necessary condition for an informed and educated society.
2. Support the creation, maintenance, and use of accurate information and support the development of information management systems which place the highest priority on accuracy and integrity.
3. Condemn and resist the unethical or immoral use or concealment of information.
4. Affirm that the collection, maintenance, distribution, and use of information about individuals is a privilege in trust: the right to privacy of all individuals must be both promoted and upheld.
5. Support compliance with statutory and regulatory laws related to recorded information.

II: The Professional Principles

Because of their responsibilities to their employers or clients as well as to their profession, information and records managers:

1. Pursue appropriate educational requirements for professional practice, including a program of ongoing education and certification.
2. Accurately represent their education, competencies, certifications, and experience to superiors, clients, co-workers and colleagues in the profession.
3. Serve the client or employer at the highest level of professional competence.
4. Recognize illegal or unethical situations and inform the client or employer of possible adverse implications.

5. Avoid personal interest or improper gain at the expense of clients, employers, or co-workers.
6. Maintain the confidentiality of privileged information.
7. Enrich the profession by sharing knowledge and experience; encourage public discussion of the profession's values, services, and skills.
8. Are actively committed to recruiting individuals to the profession on the basis of competence and educational qualifications without discrimination.

(Reproduced by permission of the Association of Records Managers and Administrators)

1.5 International Council on Archives, Code of Ethics

www.ica.org/c_ethics_e.html

[adopted by the General Assembly in its XIIIrd session in Beijing (China) on 6 September 1996]

Introduction

A. A code of ethics for archivists should establish high standards of conduct for the archival profession.
It should introduce new members of the profession to those standards, remind experienced archivists of their professional responsibilities and inspire public confidence in the profession.

B. The term archivists as used in this code is intended to encompass all those concerned with the control, care, custody, preservation and administration of archives.

C. Employing institutions and archive services should be encouraged to adopt policies and practices that facilitate the implementation of this code.

D. This code is intended to provide an ethical framework for guidance of members of the profession, and not to provide specific solutions to particular problems.

E. The principles are all accompanied by a commentary; principles and commentary taken together constitute the Code of Ethics.

F. The code is dependent upon the willingness of archival institutions and professional associations to implement it. This may take the form of an educational effort and the establishment of machinery to provide guidance in cases of doubt, to investigate unethical conduct, and if considered appropriate, to apply sanctions.

Code

1. Archivists should protect the integrity of archival material and thus guarantee that it continues to be reliable evidence of the past.

2. Archivists should appraise, select and maintain archival material in its historical, legal and administrative context, thus retaining the principle

of provenance, preserving and making evident the original relationships of documents.

3. Archivists should protect the authenticity of documents during archival processing, preservation and use.

4. Archivists should ensure the continuing accessibility and intelligibility of archival materials.

5. Archivists should record, and be able to justify, their actions on archival material.

6. Archivists should promote the widest possible access to archival material and provide an impartial service to all users.

7. Archivists should respect both access and privacy, and act within the boundaries of relevant legislation.

8. Archivists should use the special trust given to them in the general interest and avoid using their position to unfairly benefit themselves or others.

9. Archivists should pursue professional excellence by systematically and continuously updating their archival knowledge, and sharing the results of their research and experience.

10. Archivists should promote the preservation and use of the world's documentary heritage, through working co-operatively with the members of their own and other professions.

(Reproduced by permission of the International Council on Archives)

Appendix 2
Guidance documents

2.1 Internet Acceptable Use Policies

By Sally Criddle, UKOLN, on behalf of EARL, the Library
Association and UKOLN

An issue paper from the Networked Services Policy Taskgroup
Series Editor: Sarah Ormes, UKOLN
www.earl.org.uk/policy/issuepapers/internet.html

Introduction

This paper will look at how a policy for acceptable public use of the Internet
in the library can be developed and the issues affecting policy development
and implementation.

Why have an Acceptable Use Policy

The Internet has now established its place in the public library. Library staff,
and much of the general public, now appreciate its value as a provider of
information and recognise the role that public libraries have in providing
public access to the Internet. In addition, the government, in its commitment
to widening access to Information Communication Technology (ICT) and
ensuring that the benefits of the information age are open to all, recognises
the central role that public libraries have to play in ensuring that all members
of society have access to ICT and can enjoy the benefits it brings.

This recognition is being backed up by national funding programmes and
government initiatives such as the People's Network and the NOF-Digitise
programme, which are aimed at providing the networking infrastructure and
content to place public libraries at the centre of the drive to increase lifelong

learning and cultural enrichment opportunities throughout society, and to bring people into the information age, by encouraging them to use ICT.

Whilst the benefits and opportunities the Internet has to offer are becoming widely recognised and appreciated, the Internet is not without its problems, particularly in the context of use in the public library. Much is made in the media of the pornography that can be accessed on the Web and critics will cite the potentially offensive and illegal material that can be accessed as reasons why it is unsuitable for use in a public library.

To exploit the opportunities offered by the Internet and to minimise the negative aspects, public access to the Internet in the library needs to be effectively managed. Careful consideration must be given to questions such as who should have access to the Internet and under what conditions, what Internet services should be offered and with what restrictions.

An Acceptable Use Policy (AUP) is a crucial tool in helping to manage public access to the Internet. An effectively written policy will clarify the level of service that the public can expect, provide guidance for management of the medium and can communicate to the wider community the place that the Internet occupies within the public library.

Guiding principles of policy development

Ideally the AUP should be written before a public access Internet service is introduced. It should be a positive statement developed from the core values of the library service, rather than a reactive document written in response to problems that have been encountered, and should complement existing library policies. It needs to be practically enforceable, and must be supported with appropriate administrative procedures so that it can be implemented effectively by front-line library staff. All library staff must be familiar with the policy, have an understanding of why particular decisions have been made and be aware of the implications of the policy. Front-line staff should be able to explain the reasoning behind the policy and the implications for users.

The policy should be consistent with existing library policies. Examining policies that the library already has in areas such as age limits on users (if any), charges for services, video borrowing criteria etc. may provide guidance in areas of Internet access. The AUP must also be written with reference to the national policy context such as the Library Association's statements in related areas such as freedom of information and censorship and restrictions imposed by funding bodies content produced from the New Opportunities Funding programme must, for example, be free.

As well as ensuring that the Internet AUP does not conflict with existing polices, an AUP that is produced with regard to established policies will ensure that the Internet becomes an integral part of the library's existing services, and will demonstrate how it is complementing existing services rather than seeking to replace them.

Elements of an Acceptable Use Policy

What should an AUP include?

A basic AUP should address the following issues:

- Why does the library provide Internet access?
- Who will be able to use the library's Internet terminals?
- What Internet services will the library provide?
- Will access be free or charged?
- What types of resources can users access?
- Is access filtered?
- How are users expected to behave?
- How will library staff implement the AUP?

STATEMENT OF PURPOSE: Why does the library provide Internet access?
The AUP is an excellent place to set out in a clear and concise statement the role that the Internet has in the library service and the benefits it has to offer the public library. This is a good opportunity to establish the Internet as an integral part of library service provision.

PHYSICAL ACCESS: Who will be able to use the library's Internet terminals?
Once Internet terminals have been installed in the library managing the physical access to them needs to be considered. For example, will anyone be able to walk in off the street and start browsing the Web? Will access be limited to registered library users? Will passwords and user login names be used to control access?

The library could keep records of who is using the terminals (which can be particularly useful information to have if sanctions need to be enforced in the event that the AUP is transgressed). However, this needs to be balanced with the administrative overhead it will impose on staff if they are required to collect names and addresses or issue library memberships before allowing access. And users may be put off using the Internet if logging-on is seen to be time consuming and burdensome. Also, how does this fit in with policy on how other non-lending materials, such as newspapers, are used in the library? Privacy issues need consideration. Users may be uneasy about logging-on to a terminal with an identifiable password as they may think that their subsequent use and the resources they go on to browse are being recorded and could be traced back to them.

The level of demand and number of terminals that can be provided will also have a bearing on whether users are required to pre-book sessions or access is limited during busy periods.

Access for disabled users can be addressed in an AUP and the library should consider whether it would be appropriate to provide assistive technologies such as speech synthesisers or wheelchair access to terminals.

Charging for Internet access provokes much debate and many different solutions. Some libraries charge all users to access the Internet; others provide free access to a limited range of Web sites and services or charge particular users such as local businesses for access; others provide access to all services and content free of charge. Careful thought and consideration of the implications and consequences of free vs. fee access is needed. Whilst there is no definitive legislation in this area (libraries must still rely on the 1964 Public Library and Museums Act for the definition of which public library services must by law be provided free) it should be noted that the NOF-Digitise programme makes it a requirement that all content developed as a result of its funding must be provided free of charge to users of the People's Network and the National Grid for Learning. The issues of charging for access are discussed in a previous Issue Paper in this series Charging and Networked Services[1].

SERVICES: What Internet services and resources will be provided?
The World Wide Web may be the most widely used Internet service, but the AUP should also address other Internet services such as e-mail, newsgroups, chat rooms and telnet. Will access to these services be provided? If e-mail facilities are provided will incoming and outgoing mail be allowed? Can

users access free mail services such as HotMail? Will downloading of software and file transfers be allowed? Will users be required to have their own disks scanned for viruses before use?

Some libraries may not want the Internet being used for games or chat, particularly if such use ties up terminals for long periods of time (although limiting the length of sessions could help with this). Also, chat rooms and bulletin boards are often associated with sexually explicit or offensive material.

Whilst it may be tempting to prohibit use of chat rooms for entertainment purposes, it is worth considering that not all games can be dismissed as purely entertainment, some do have educational elements. Similarly, not all chat room discussions can be dismissed as frivolous. Some libraries promote virtual support groups for people with disabilities for example, or actively encourage users to form book reading groups supported by e-mail and chat rooms.

With the growth in e-commerce on the Web the AUP may need to address the commercial activities that users get involved in and it may be decided to take steps to ensure that users activities cannot incur costs to the library.

FILTERING: Does the library filter Internet access?
Are filters installed on the library's public access terminals? There are many reasons for and against the use of filters (as addressed in a previous Issue Paper – An Introduction to Filtering[2]) and the policy should include a statement on the decision that is taken.

ACCEPTABLE USE: How are users expected to behave?
The quantity and quality of resources available on the Internet has been well reported in the media, with much coverage given to the questionable and illegal materials that are available. Whilst a determined user may still be able to view offensive, illegal or other inappropriate material even if filtering software is installed, an effective AUP can make it clear that such behaviour will not be tolerated and will give staff the authority and confidence to stop it.

Example Internet AUP
Midshire Library Service provides access to a wide range of resources including those available from the Internet in its role as a provider of informational, educational, recreational and cultural enrichment opportunities for its users.

Midshire Library Service provides free access to its Internet services for all library members.

The Internet is a global electronic network and Midshire Library Service is not responsible for the accuracy, validity, legality or usefulness of information available.

Transmission of any material in violation of any laws is prohibited. This includes, but is not limited to: copyrighted material, threatening or obscene material, pornographic material, or material protected by trade secret. Use for any commercial purpose is also prohibited.

Permission of parents or guardians is required before children can use the Internet and the Library encourages parents/guardians to supervise their children's use of the Internet.

Midshire Library Service provides its members with access to the World Wide Web. The Library does not provide e-mail accounts, Internet Relay Chat or Newsgroups. Printing and downloading services are not currently available.

Whilst there is legislation such as the Obscene Publications Act[3] to guide on what might constitute illegal materials, it is very much up to individual libraries to define just what are and what are not appropriate materials to access in the public library. This is not an easy task, particularly as it can be so subjective. What one person finds totally innocuous, another person may find deeply offensive depending on their cultural or religious background, for example. One way to address this issue is (again) to consider library policy in other areas. For example, materials of an offensive nature, be they sexual, racist or violent, could be seen as creating an atmosphere of harassment which could breach existing policies on harassment or discrimination.

As well as offensive materials, the AUP should draw users attention to the fact that the authenticity and accuracy of many of the resources available over the Internet are questionable. As the law currently stands it is unlikely that a library itself would be responsible if users breach copyright, intellectual property rights or are involved in illegal activities on the Internet in the library. However, the situation needs to be made clear to users, and they should be made aware that they have a personal responsibility to abide by the relevant legislation, just as they do when photocopying copyrighted materials. The AUP should include a statement making it clear that the library is not responsible for Internet content, its authenticity or accuracy. Copyright issues are addressed in a previous Issue Paper – Copyright and the

Networked Environment[4].

The library also needs to be aware of issues of freedom of access to information, particularly if filtering Internet access. This is an area where legislation is still being determined, but the Library Association makes it clear in its statement on intellectual freedom and censorship[5] that libraries should be aiming to provide access to all publicly available information, regardless of format, for all their users.

CHILDREN'S USE: Children's access to the Internet deserves particular consideration. It is usual for parents/guardians to be asked to provide their consent before their children can use the Internet. A consent form could incorporate the terms and conditions under which access is provided for children. Some libraries choose to install filters on Internet terminals only in the children's library; others make it explicit that parents/guardians are responsible for the material that their children view and that the library has no responsibility for supervising access by children. Providing links to materials for children and sites that have been selected as being particularly suitable for children are good ways of guiding use.

The AUP can draw on the library's existing policies on provision of services to children. Aligning children's access to the Internet with existing policy on, for example, the categories of books and videos that they can borrow, will help to demonstrate how the Internet fits in with services already provided by the library. Whatever level of access is provided, it must be clearly defined in the policy.

POLICY INTO PRACTICE: How will library staff implement the AUP?
All library staff should be aware of the AUP and have an understanding of the issues that it addresses and the implications that the policy will have on public use. There should be appropriate administrative procedures in place so that the policy can be implemented effectively. An AUP can also be very useful in dealing with enquiries from, for example, local councillors or journalists about how the Internet is being used in the library.

Although this paper focuses on acceptable use by the public, staff use should also be considered. Will access for them be under the same conditions as for the public? The local authority may already have a policy for Internet access by employees or the public policy could form the basis of a council-wide policy.

A statement about the level of assistance and guidance that users can expect from library staff could be included in the AUP. If resources for assisting the public are limited, providing support in the form of lists of resources and links to subject guides, such as EARLweb,[7] can be very effective.

Users must be made aware of the terms and conditions under which the library is providing Internet access. The AUP should be prominently displayed near Internet terminals. One way of highlighting the policy is to display it as a front screen on the Internet terminals: users must click on the screen before they can proceed, to confirm that they have read and will comply with the policy.

The policy should be clear on the consequences for users who breach the conditions. This is usually dealt with by Internet use being withdrawn or restricted.

Finally, as with any policy, the AUP should be reviewed periodically. The policy needs to be workable on a day-to-day basis and should reflect changes in this area of rapid technological development, where society's familiarity with the Internet is increasing day by day.

Policy Challenges[6]

An interesting exercise, once an AUP has been drafted, is to see how well the policy deals with various hypothetical situations such as:

- The library's mission statement states that the library aims to provide the most effective information service that it can to meet the information needs of all of its users and will try to get hold of any legal material requested a user complains that this statement is blatantly irreconcilable with the library's use of filters.
- A parent in the library notices that in clear view of the children's library someone is looking at a pornographic site the parent makes a complaint how will the library deal with it?
- Someone who has used one of the library's terminals used information they found on the Internet to make some investments the information was out of date and the user lost some money and claims the library is responsible for providing incorrect information.

References

1 Charging and Networked Services
   http://www.earl.org.uk/policy/issuepapers/charging.html
2 An Introduction to Filtering
   http://www.earl.org.uk/policy/issuepapers/filtering.html
3 See, for example, the Obscene Publications Act 1959, the Protection of Children Act 1978 and the Criminal Justice and Public Order Act 1994.
4 Copyright and the Networked Environment
   http://www.earl.org.uk/policy/issuepapers/copyright.html
5 Library Association statement on Intellectual Freedom and Censorship
   http://www.la-hq.org.uk/directory/prof_issues/ifac.html
   [Note: for any updates see www.cilip.org.uk]
6 Policy Challenges
   www.ukoln.ac.uk/public/present/nag/challenges.htm
7 EARLweb
   http://www.earl.org.uk/earlweb/index.html

Other relevant resources

Smith, M. Internet policy handbook for librarians.
   New York: Neal-Schuman, 1999.
Safe Surfin guidance for children's use of the Internet
   http://www.safesurfin.com/
Examples from UK public library AUPs
   http://www.ukoln.ac.uk/public/present/nag/policies.htm

Acknowledgements

This is one of a series of issue papers which will be produced by the EARL Networked Services Policy Taskgroup. UKOLN, the Library Association and EARL member libraries participate in the taskgroup. Queries about the issue papers series should be addressed to Penny Garrod, the project manager for the initiative:

Penny Garrod, UKOLN, The University of Bath, Bath BA1 7AY
E-mail: p.garrod@ukoln.ac.uk
Telephone: 01225 826711

UKOLN is funded by the Library & Information Commission, the Joint Information Systems Committee of the Higher Education Funding Councils, as well as by project funding from the JISC's Electronic Libraries Programme and the European Union. UKOLN also receives support from the University of Bath where it is based.

(Reproduced by permission of UKOLN and
CILIP: the Chartered Institute of Library and Information Professionals)

2.2 An introduction to filtering

By Sarah Ormes, UKOLN, on behalf of EARL, the Library Association and UKOLN

An issue paper from the Networked Services Policy Taskgroup
Series Editor: Sarah Ormes, UKOLN
www.ukoln.ac.uk/public/earl/issuepapers/filtering.html

What is filtering?

Filtering is the term used to describe the use of software which restricts access to material on the Internet. Such software is often used as a method to try to prevent access to pornography and other potentially offensive material.

How does filtering software work?

Filtering software works in three main ways:

- Keyword blocking
- Site blocking
- Web rating systems

Keyword blocking

Filtering packages which use keyword blocking have a list of 'forbidden words' which they search for in web pages, e-mail messages or even Internet Relay Chat and other 'chat' functions. If the software finds those words it will either prevent the user from accessing those e-mail messages or pages or block out the relevant sections of it. The list of 'forbidden words' may initially be set by the software provider although some filtering packages will allow additional words to be added by the software purchaser.

Site blocking

Filtering software packages which use site blocking have a list of sites which they will not allow access to. This list typically consists of pornography and other potentially offensive sites. The list of sites is drawn up by the software

provider although usually there is an option for the software purchaser to add
to it. Updates to this list of sites can usually be downloaded regularly from
the software provider. Filtering packages working on this principle can also
be set up to allow access only to a list of certain stipulated sites. Some of the
software packages will also allow you to edit the list of 'banned' sites.

Increasingly, filtering packages use both site blocking and keyword
blocking.

Web rating systems

A recent development has been the creation of web rating systems. These
systems are actually built into the web pages and web browsers themselves.
The most well known is called PICS (Platform for Internet Content Selection)[1] which is being developed by the World Wide Web Consortium (W3C).

The system works through web sites being rated in terms of the nudity,
violence, sex and language used in them. These ratings can either be
embedded in the web page itself or managed by a third party rating bureau.
The web browser is then set to accept only pages which are rated at certain
levels e.g. no nudity allowed but mild expletives accepted. Organisations like
RSACi (Recreational Software Advisory Council on the Internet)[2] are already
acting as third party rating bureaux and other organisations such as Internet
Service Providers (ISPs) and filtering software companies are also developing
these services.

RSACi Ratings for Language

Level 0: inoffensive slang
Level 1: mild expletives
Level 2: moderate expletives
Level 3: obscene gestures
Level 4: explicit or crude language

How well does filtering software work?

Karen Schneider's Internet Filter Assessment Project[3] evaluated how
effective commercial filtering software was. Volunteer librarians gathered a
collection of real reference queries and tried to answer them using

workstations which did and did not have filtering software installed.

Her research found that the current generation of filters were not completely effective. They either blocked out information which was required to answer typical reference queries or did not block material which was considered by the testers to be very offensive. Filters which operated by keyword blocking alone were found to be especially ineffective:

> Over 35% of the time, the filters blocked some information they needed to answer a question. Keyword blocking obscured everything from nursery rhymes ('pussycat, pussycat' – blocked repeatedly, even, in one case, when the tester used the search terms 'nursery rhymes') to government physics archives (the URL began with XXX) to the word 'button'.
>
> Eight percent of what testers accessed they determined was 'objectionable' . . . filters can't block what they don't know about.

In conclusion, she found that filters were not completely reliable as yet. They did not block all offensive material and on a fairly regular basis prevented access to inoffensive and useful material. However, filters are still in a state of development and are becoming more sophisticated.

Other solutions like web rating systems are also still in an early stage of development and are too under used to be relied upon yet. Very few web sites have yet implemented PICS and general awareness of it is low but looks set to grow. Already some national governments are interested in the system and may soon be promoting it.

Why is it an issue for libraries?

Increasingly, public libraries are providing their users with access to the Internet. Some of the concerns librarians have identified about providing public access Internet services are that:

- Users will deliberately access and view pornography
- Children could also gain access to pornography
- The library will, by default, be providing access to illegal material

The following section looks at some of the pros and cons of the use of filtering software in public libraries. Many of the examples drawn upon are from the experience of American public libraries. This reflects their greater experience of providing public access Internet services compared to many UK libraries.

Pros of using filtering software

Providing for users' needs

Public libraries have always had stock selection policies which guide them in selecting the best and most suitable resources for their library users. Libraries generally will not stock material that is not 'suitable' (typically, pornographic and/or potentially offensive). Providing unfiltered access to the Internet could negate the library's role in providing access to a pre-selected and organised collection.

Children and pornography

There is a possibility that children may accidentally be able to gain access to pornography and other potentially offensive and/or illegal material through the library's Internet workstations. David Burt of Filtering Facts[4] argues that:

> The community entrusts its children to be safe in the library. The community assumes that the library has some minimum standards for what types of materials a child might encounter at the library. The community will not trust the library to be a safe place for children if it becomes the equivalent of an adult bookstore. Pornography and children have no business with one another, especially not in a public library.

If libraries are to maintain their perceived role as a 'safe place' for children in the community they will need to address the concerns parents may have about their children accessing pornography over the Internet. Using filtering software is one way to address these concerns and try to ensure the safety of children using public library Internet resources.

Maria's Peace of Mind

Maria's children really want to use the Internet in the nearby public library for some of their homework projects. Maria is worried about them using it as she keeps reading in the paper about the amount of pornography that is available on the Internet and how easy it is to find. When she asks the librarian in the library about this she is told that the library uses filtering software which will ensure that her children will be completely safe when they use the Internet and will only be able to see 'suitable' material. She is reassured by this and is now happy for her kids to use the Internet.

Legal issues

Libraries in the USA have had to face legal challenges when they do not use filtering software and users of the library have been exposed to 'offensive material' through library Internet connections.

In May 1998 Livermore Public Library, California became the first public library to be sued for failing to protect children from pornography.[5] The complaint was filed by a parent who claimed that a minor accessed sexually explicit web sites using the library's computers, downloaded images harmful to minors to a floppy disk, and then printed them out at a relative's house.

Cons of using filtering software

Freedom of access to information

There have been several well publicised instances of public libraries in America being prosecuted by the American Civil Liberties Union (ACLU) because of their use of filtering software.[6] The ACLU and also the American Library Association[7] argue that public libraries should provide unfiltered access to the Internet in order to maintain and uphold America's first amendment right to seek and receive all types of information, from all points of view. Libraries should provide access to the Internet with the same constitutional protections that apply to the books on library shelves.

In Britain the Library Association states in its statement on intellectual freedom and censorship[8] that:

> The function of a library or information service is to provide, as far as resources allow, all publicly available information in which its users claim legitimate interest. Such provision should be regardless of format and include factual and fiction material. The materials, electronic information services, networks and other facilities provided directly or indirectly by the library or information service should be equally accessible to all users. Those who provide library or information services should not restrict this access except as required by law.

However, it should be noted that the Library Association has not yet drafted a specific policy about the use of filtering software in libraries. It is expected that such a policy will be developed in late 1998. [Note: The Library Association produced a policy statement, *The use of filtering software in libraries*, in 1999, followed by guidance notes in 2000. See **www.la-hq.org.uk/directory/ prof_issues/filter.html**. For any updates see **www.cilip.org.uk**.]

Who decides what is filtered?

The use of filters often involves an outside organisation developing a list of 'acceptable and unacceptable' sites. Traditionally, stock selection has been seen as a task for professionally trained staff. By accepting lists of banned sites libraries are passing over the assessment of what is and isn't suitable material for their users to an outside organisation. These assessments may not necessarily be made with the sophistication and awareness which trained librarians apply in stock selection activities.

The role of the library

The public library could be the only place where some users will be able to access the Internet. Their information needs may not necessarily map onto those used by filters and their one potential source of networked information will therefore be unusable.

Legal issues

By offering 'filtered' access to the Internet public libraries could be seen as stating that they guarantee a 'safe Internet environment' for their users. As Karen Schneider's research has shown filters are not yet 100% effective and a completely 'safe' Internet environment cannot yet be achieved. There is a danger that libraries could therefore be putting themselves into a position where they are liable for legal action when filters do not screen out inappropriate material.

David's Information Needs

David is 18 and thinks he is gay. He wants to find out about 'coming out' and talk to someone who will be able to give him advice and support. He saw a programme on television last night about coming out which gave details about a web site which looked really interesting and useful. He doesn't have access at home and so will need to use the Internet terminals in the public library. He finds a free one in the corner where no one can easily see his screen and types in the URL of the site - he gets an access denied message. He wants to know why he is getting this message but is too embarrassed to ask. He leaves the library disappointed.

Whether you filter or don't filter – have a policy!

Irrespective of whether libraries choose to use filtering software or not it is important that they develop a policy about it.

Many of these types of policies have already been developed by public libraries around the world.[9] They often vary in their detail but will generally state what users are allowed to do when using the library's Internet resources. For example, a policy may state that the Internet can only be used as a research tool i.e. not for 'chatting' or games and that parents must sign a form agreeing that they are happy for their child to use the library's Internet resources. It may also state that the library cannot be held responsible for the type of material that may be found on the Internet and that parents are responsible for supervising their child's use of the Internet.

As libraries have developed policies on most areas of their service it is important that they do so on the topic of public access Internet services. Part of that policy must be a decision about whether they implement filtering software or not. Whatever their decision it must be one that they are able to defend and explain to their users.

Example of a Library Internet Access Policy

The Bloggshire Public Library Service provides public access to the Internet in keeping with its role as a source of information, intellectual development, and enrichment for the community.

The Bloggshire Public Library Service has no control over the information accessed and cannot be held responsible for the content or quality of the information retrieved.

Transmission of any material in violation of any laws is prohibited. This includes, but is not limited to: copyrighted material, threatening or obscene material, pornographic material, or material protected by trade secret. Use for any commercial purpose is also prohibited.

As is the case with all other library materials, any restriction of a child's access to the Internet is the responsibility of the child's parent or legal guardian.

Due to our limited resources, we reserve the right to restrict Internet access to research and information sources only.

References

1 PICS **http://www.w3.org/PICS/**
2 RSACi **http://www.rsac.org/homepage.asp**
3 The Internet Filter Assessment Project
   http://www.bluehighways.com/tifap/
4 Filtering Facts **http://www.filteringfacts.org/**
5 Livermore Public Library Court Case
6 ACLU Court Case **http://www.aclu.org/news/n040798a.html**
7 American Library Association Statement on Library Use of Filtering Software
   http://www.ala.org/alaorg/oif/filt_stm.html
8 Library Association Statement on Intellectual Freedom and Censorship
   http://www.la-hq.org.uk/directory/prof_issues/ifac.html
   [Note: for any updates see **www.cilip.org.uk**]
9 Public Library Internet Access Policies
   http://www.ci.oswego.or.us/library/poli.htm

Other relevant resources

A collection of resources about filtering can be found at:
   http://www.rcls.org/libland/cen/cens.htM
The American Library Association's web page about the Internet and intellectual freedom can be found at:
   http://www.ala.org/alaorg/oif/filtersandfiltering.html
A mailing list about filtering called FILT4LIB can be found at:
   filt4lib@public.ci.escondido.ca.us
   To subscribe to it you need to send an e-mail with the word 'subscribe' in the subject field, and nothing in the message field.
The Loudoun software censoring case. Loudoun County, VA censorware lawsuit can be found at:
   http://censorware.org/legal/loudoun

Acknowledgements

This is one of a series of issue papers which will be produced by the EARL Networked Services Policy Taskgroup. UKOLN, the Library Association and EARL member libraries participate in the taskgroup. Queries about the issue papers series should be addressed to Penny Garrod, the project manager for the initiative:

Penny Garrod, UKOLN, The University of Bath, Bath BA1 7AY
E-mail: pgarrod@ukoln.ac.uk
Telephone: 01225 826711

UKOLN is funded by the Library & Information Commission, the Joint Information Systems Committee of the Higher Education Funding Councils, as well as by project funding from the JISC's Electronic Libraries Programme and the European Union. UKOLN also receives support from the University of Bath where it is based.

(Reproduced by permission of UKOLN and
CILIP: the Chartered Institute of Library and Information Professionals)

2.3 Guidelines for Parents
www.missingkids.com

By taking responsibility for your children's online computer use, parents can greatly minimize any potential risks of being online. Make it a family rule to

- Never give out identifying information — home address, school name, or telephone number — in a public message such as chat or bulletin boards (newsgroup), and be sure you're dealing with someone both you and your children know and trust before giving out this information via E-mail. Think carefully before revealing any personal information such as age, marital status, or financial information. Do not post photographs of your children on web sites or in newsgroups that are available to the public. Consider using a pseudonym, avoid listing your child's name and E-mail address in any public directories and profiles, and find out about your ISP's privacy policies and exercise your options for how your personal information may be used.
- Get to know the Internet and any services your child uses. If you don't know how to log on, get your child to show you. Have your child show you what he or she does online, and become familiar with all the things that you can do online.
- Never allow a child to arrange a face-to-face meeting with another computer user without parental permission. If a meeting is arranged, make the first one in a public place, and be sure to accompany your child.
- Never respond to messages or bulletin-board items that are suggestive, obscene, belligerent, threatening, or make you feel uncomfortable. Encourage your children to tell you if they encounter such messages. If you or your child receives a message that is harassing, of a sexual nature, or threatening, forward a copy of the message to your ISP, and ask for their assistance. Instruct your child **not** to click on any links that are contained in E-mail from persons they don't know. Such links could lead to sexually explicit or otherwise inappropriate web sites.

  If someone sends you or your children messages or images that are obscene, lewd, filthy, or indecent with the intent to harass, abuse, annoy, or threaten, or if you become aware of the transmission, use, or viewing of child pornography while online, immediately report this to the National Center for Missing & Exploited Children's CyberTipline at 1-800-843-5678 or www.cybertipline.com.

- Remember that people online may not be who they seem. Because you can't see or even hear the person it would be easy for someone to misrepresent him- or herself. Thus, someone indicating that 'she' is a '12-year-old girl' could in reality be a 40-year-old man.
- Remember that everything you read online may not be true. Any offer that's 'too good to be true' probably is. Be careful about any offers that involve you coming to a meeting, having someone visit your house, or sending money or credit-card information.
- Set reasonable rules and guidelines for computer use by your children. (See 'My Rules for Online Safety' on the back cover.) Discuss these rules and post them near the computer as a reminder. Remember to monitor your children's compliance with these rules, especially when it comes to the amount of time your children spend on the computer. A child's excessive use of online services or the Internet, especially late at night, may be a clue that there is a potential problem. Remember that personal computers and online services should not be used as electronic babysitters.
- Check out blocking, filtering, and ratings. Be sure to make this a family activity. Consider keeping the computer in a family room rather than the child's bedroom. Get to know their 'online friends' just as you get to know all of their other friends.

(Extracted from the brochure *Child Safety on the Information Highway*, in accordance with the reprint policy of the National Center for Missing and Exploited Children.)

2.4 Staying Safe Online: A Young Person's Contract
www.getnetwise.org/tools/toolscontracts.shtml

1. I will ALWAYS tell a parent or another adult immediately, if something is confusing or seems scary or threatening.
2. I will NEVER give out my full name, real address, telephone number, school name or location, schedule, password, or other identifying information when I'm online. I will check with an adult for any exceptions.
3. I will NEVER have a face-to-face meeting with someone I've met online. In rare cases, my parents may decide it's OK, but if I do decide to meet a cyberpal, I will make sure we meet in a public place and that a parent or guardian is with me.
4. I will NEVER respond online to any messages that use bad words or words that are scary, threatening, or just feel weird. If I get that kind of message, I'll print it out and tell an adult immediately. The adult can then contact the online service or appropriate agency. If I'm uncomfortable in a live chat room, I will use the 'ignore' button.
5. I will NEVER go into a new online area that is going to cost additional money without first asking permission from my parent or teacher.
6. I will NEVER send a picture over the Internet or via regular mail to anyone without my parent's permission.
7. I will NOT give out a credit card number online without a parent present.

Young Person_____ Date_____
Parent/Guardian_____ Date_____

(Reproduced by permission of the Children's Partnership and GetNetWise)

Appendix 3
Internal policy documents

3.1 Birmingham City Council internet usage policy

Introduction

Internet access is a corporate IT service provided to help you do your job. This policy sits within a framework of City Council strategies and current Government legislation, including the Human Rights Act, which became law in October 2000. It aims to make Internet usage in Birmingham City Council both cost-effective and secure and replaces an earlier version, operational since 1997. **The policy applies to employees, contractors working for the Council and to elected members.**

What are the objectives of this policy ?

- To encourage Internet usage, where this supports the electronic delivery of Council services, and to minimise security risks to information resources and IT equipment.
- To support the Council's equal opportunities and related policies, by preventing access to web sites which display sexually-explicit, racist or other inappropriate material.
- To encourage a culture of personal responsibility amongst managers and staff, so that limited private Internet use is allowed, but effective use of resources is maintained and fair and appropriate levels of monitoring are carried out.
- To recover the corporate costs of providing Internet access within a network connection charge (per PC), not via an explicit Internet subscription.

How does this policy relate to other corporate IT strategies and policies ?

The City Council's new corporate IT strategy recognises the need for increased electronic contact with customers and business partners. Government expectations are driving this process forward and the Internet will increasingly become a primary access point for requesting Council services and a communication channel for officers delivering them.

An environment where the Council's WAN interconnects with other networks and is accessible by large numbers of customers demands a clear and effective network security policy. This Internet usage policy is therefore an integral part of the City's corporate security policies. These cover information resources and IT and communications equipment, and are being implemented to ensure the City Council complies with British Standard BS7799 . . . Code of Practice for Information Security Management.

What does the policy allow ?

- **Universal access** All Council employees and elected members are allowed to use the Internet for business purposes, if they have a valid user id and password. All officers must sign the request form (page 4) confirming the legitimate business need and that they have accepted the terms of this policy.
- **Personal access control** Individual user ids and passwords must be kept confidential and not disclosed to other staff or the public.
- **Limited private use** The Council acknowledges that Internet access is fast becoming a business tool equivalent to the telephone and e-mail, and that all such tools are sometimes used for non work-related reasons. Limited private use by legitimate Internet users is therefore being allowed and all usage (both business-related and private) will be monitored by CNS and reviewed by the Corporate Security Group, which represents all Departments. It is recommended that private use be conducted outside core office hours, though individual Departmental managers can agree local variations to this arrangement.
- **File transfers** Downloading of files from the Internet for legitimate Council business is allowed (provided Departmental IT Groups have given prior approval) but care should be taken to check for embedded

viruses. Large files (over 20Mb) should only be downloaded out of core hours. Uploading files from the WAN is allowed under special circumstances by arrangement with Corporate Network Services (CNS).

- **Secure data communications** Sensitive data may be transferred across the Internet but must be encrypted. Guidance on encryption can be found in the Council's network security policy or from CNS.
- **Newsgroups** Access to newsgroups is allowed where there is a legitimate business need and can be arranged by CNS.

What the policy does NOT allow ?

- Independent dial-up (modem) or other connections to the Internet (or to any external organisation) are not allowed from networked PCs or servers. Such connections must be physically isolated from the WAN, unless the connections have been explicitly authorised by CNS. Internet connections using the Council's telephone network are also not allowed.
- No attempt must be made to disable, defeat or circumvent City Council firewalls or similar network security facilities.
- The display of any kind of sexually-explicit image or document on any Council system is a violation of Council policy on sexual harassment. In addition, sexually-explicit material may not be stored, distributed, edited or recorded using the WAN or any computing resources. In exceptional circumstances, and when requested by a Departmental Director, access to such material will be authorised by the Head of CNS for Council officers to carry out specific duties.
- Internet facilities must not be used to break the law. Use of any IT resources for illegal activity is grounds for immediate dismissal and the Council will co-operate with any law enforcement agency in such situations.
- Internet facilities must not be used to download entertainment software or games, and users must not play games over the Internet.
- Departmental IT groups must give prior approval before any software is downloaded. Any downloaded software must be for direct business use, be properly licensed and immediately added to Departmental inventories and asset registers. No pirated software or data may be downloaded or distributed. All files downloaded via the Internet become the property of the Council, unless otherwise agreed by the relevant Departmental IT manager.

- No employee, Council contractor or elected member may use Internet facilities to deliberately propagate any virus, worm, Trojan horse or trap-door program code.
- No software or data owned or licensed to the City Council can be uploaded without **explicit** authorisation from the manager responsible for that software or data.
- The Council's firewall software will automatically disconnect Internet connections after an inactive period of 30 minutes, to prevent unauthorised use of machines that have been inadvertently left logged on. Users should not leave PCs signed on when unattended.
- **Any Internet user who knowingly contravenes any of the above is liable to disciplinary action.**

How and why is Internet (and email) usage monitored ?

The City Council uses special software to prevent access to unauthorised sites, to authenticate users, to monitor which web sites they visit and any file transfers made, and to monitor email. Web trends are analysed from detailed monitoring data, showing popular sites, lengths of time spent browsing and attempts to access unauthorised sites.

Monitoring and interception systems allow an individual's web usage to be analysed in great detail, which enables this usage policy to be enforced when necessary. Detailed analysis of an individual's use of the Internet will only be carried out in response to a formal request from a Departmental Director or the City's Internal Audit section. Such a procedure would follow the same principles as for a detailed analysis of telephone call logs. In such cases, files stored anywhere on the WAN may be inspected in order to ensure compliance with the policy.

Internet usage monitoring is an essential part of protecting the Council's business interests and, as electronic delivery of services increases, the integrity of those services. It is also an important element of planning future commun-ications requirements. The monitoring and interception of electronic com-munications is permitted if carried out in accordance with the Lawful Business Practice Regulations issued under the Regulation of Investigatory Powers Act 2000. These Regulations provide that any interception must be for one or more of a number of stated purposes relevant to the conduct of the business and that all those using the (internet/email) system must be notified of the fact.

BIRMINGHAM CITY COUNCIL

Request for Access to the Internet for City Council Employees

Please complete ALL sections, and in block capitals.

Name...

Current Network User ID..

Position...

Division/section..

Department..

Location...

Tel number..............................

Reason(s) for Internet Access

I have received a copy of the City Council's Internet Usage Policy, which I have read in conjunction with any IT usage policies produced by my own Department. I fully understand the terms of the Council's Internet Usage Policy and agree to abide by them. I realise that the Council's security software may record, for management use, the Internet address of any site that I visit and keep a record of any network activity in which I transmit or receive any kind of file. I acknowledge that any message I send or receive may be recorded and stored in an archive file for management use. I know that any violation of this policy could lead to disciplinary action or even criminal prosecution.

This document will be kept on my Departmental Personnel File

Signed................................... Date..................

Approved by

Line manager (print).......................................
Line manager (sign)............................. Date..................

Copies of this approval must be kept by both of the above signatories and the original sent to your Departmental Systems Section for action. No access to the Internet will be granted without this approval.

INTERNET USAGE - Best Practice

- All Internet usage should be conducted honestly, respecting copyrights, software licensing rules, property rights etc as in other business dealings. Other relevant Council policies apply to Internet usage, especially in terms of privacy, misuse of resources, sexual harassment, security and confidentiality.
- Private Internet usage must be in employees' own time and kept to a minimum. All usage is monitored (including private use) and future service reviews may look at instances of excessive usage.
- Employees, authorised to speak to the media or in public, may contribute to chat rooms and newsgroups in the name of the City Council. Other employees should participate as individuals, speaking only for themselves. All employees should refrain from political advocacy or the endorsement of commercial products or services. Specific advice in this area should be sought from the Communications & Customer Relations Division (303-4941).
- Chats, newsgroups and e-mail facilities give users an immense reach to propagate corporate City Council messages. Special care should be taken to maintain the clarity, consistency and integrity of the Council's corporate image. An individual's e-mail or posting may be taken as the Council's corporate position. It is recommended that users forgo a measure of their individual freedom when participating in chats or newsgroups on Council business. Confidential Council information and customer data must not be distributed by the Internet and employees are reminded that such actions, even if inadvertent, may contravene Council security policies.
- Internet users must identify themselves honestly, accurately and completely (including Council affiliation and function where requested) when participating in chat rooms or newsgroups, or when setting up accounts on external computer systems.
- The City Council retains the copyright to original material posted to any forum, newsgroup, chat or Web page by any employee in the course of his or her duties.

- Unnecessary Internet usage causes network and server congestion, slows other users and ties up printers and other shared resources. Unlawful Internet usage may result in negative publicity for the Council and expose it to significant legal liabilities.
- Schedule any communications-intensive operations (eg large file transfers, video downloads, mass e-mails) **outside core time** ie before 10.00 or after 16.00. Video and audio streaming and downloading technologies represent significant data traffic, which often causes local network congestion. Video and audio material downloaded must be for explicit business use.
- **Before** downloaded files are run or accessed, they must be scanned for viruses, using memory-resident or network virus checking software such as Sophos Sweep for Netware or Sophos Intercheck for Windows.

Within this policy:
Council includes all City Council Departments, offices and locations, including schools
Document includes any file, readable on a computer screen, as if it were a printed page
Graphics includes photographs, pictures, animations, movies, or drawings
Display includes monitors, flat-panel active or passive matrix displays, LCDs, projectors, televisions and virtual-reality tools.

(By permission of Birmingham City Council)

3.2 A County Library, Public Access to the Internet: Notes of Guidance for Library Staff

Preamble

The introduction of a service giving public access to the Internet is the first in a wave of ICT related services which will be introduced over the next year. Other services being planned include public access catalogues at all service points (including mobiles), a Countywide Community Information System and public access to office software such as word-processing and spreadsheets. Increased use of CD ROMs will also be possible. Over the coming months, libraries will receive further PCs to allow them to provide more access points to the Internet and to help deliver the other new services (the actual number will vary from Iibrary to library).

Internet access

This service providing public access to the Internet is designed to complement, enhance and increase the range of information already provided at our service points. The service is available to everyone, whether members of a library or not, as long as they are willing to observe and agree to our Internet policy. In addition, the Internet is used by some library staff in answering enquiries from the community.

Through this service, members of the public have:

- access to the World Wide Web and the millions of sites which it already holds
- web-based email (eg Yahoo, Hotmail)
- access to discussion groups/newsgroups

Policy

The Conditions of Use outlined below form part of the County Library's policy on Public Access to the Internet and must be enforced by Library staff at all times. All members of the public who book Internet sessions are expected to observe them and have to sign to that effect. (These conditions are available in poster form – permanently on display in each library – and as handouts so that all users are fully informed).

1. This service is provided to give access to the World Wide Web and to web-based email facilities.
2. In order to manage demand, a booking system is in place. Users must book in order to be allocated a session and must observe the time limits set by the staff.
3. Users must not cause any damage to the hardware or software and must not violate the security of the system or change system configurations.
4. Users may download material to floppy disk only. These disks must be purchased from library staff at each booked session (Use of disks which they have brought with them will carry a risk of introducing viruses to our system). Users' downloading of material to the hard disk has been barred.
5. Printouts of downloaded material are subject to a charge which must be paid to library staff at the time of use.
6. All copyright laws must be observed. A poster summarising copyright requirements is on display in each library.
7. The transmission of any materials which contravene the law is strictly forbidden, as is the use of Library Internet terminals for any commercial purpose. This condition includes, but is not limited to, the sale and purchase of goods and services and the transmission of material which is judged to be extremist, threatening, obscene or libellous.

Any individual whose actions contravene library service policy or these Conditions of Use will be barred from further use of the facility or from use of the library service as a whole. Group Librarians will consider the details of each case separately with reference to the Public Services Librarian as necessary.

Disclaimers

The County Library is providing an Internet service to improve the range and quantity of information which is available to the public. No filtering system is in operation, so there is uncontrolled access to the Internet. However, members of the public must observe the Conditions of Use (see above). We cannot assume responsibility for the following and this will be made clear to all users **who must be made aware of our policy statement (Conditions of Use) before they access the Internet on library PCs.** Use is at the user's own risk.

1. The County Library does not monitor, and has no control over, the content of Internet sites. We cannot take responsibility for the content.
2. Not all sites provide accurate, current or complete information. Users must exercise their own judgement.
3. The speed and success of users' searches cannot be guaranteed.
4. The availability of Internet facilities and sites on any particular day cannot be guaranteed as problems may arise due to technical difficulties, high levels of demand etc.
5. No filtering takes place, so material which some people may find offensive is accessible if people abuse the service.
6. Virus checking software is installed on PCs, but protection cannot be guaranteed.
7. The County Library cannot be held responsible for any loss of data, damage or liability that may occur from use of a library's computer.

Censorship

If material does not contravene the law, then library users can legitimately expect to be allowed access to it. Agreement to our Conditions of Use should mean that members of the public access only sites whose content is legal. We have always recognised, with the support of the Library Association, that it is not the job of library staff to act as censors.

All PCs should be sited where the screen can be seen easily by staff and other library users. This, in itself, will restrict the types of material which most people will seek to access.

Use of the Internet by children under the age of 18 will only be allowed with the permission of their parent or guardian.

Children

Parents are entirely responsible for the use of the Internet by their own children and only they can restrict access. Children (under the age of 18) will not be able to use the service unless their parent has signed a consent form which will give their child total access. Parental approval will lead to staff issuing the child with a 'viewer card' which must be produced on each occasion. Library staff will not intervene when children have their parents' approval.

The nature of some of the material on the Internet will he made clear to parents to enable them to make an appropriate decision about the degree of access which they are willing to allow their child.

Parents will be encouraged to accompany their children when they are making use of the Internet and to supervise them closely.

Copyright

Material on the World Wide Web is protected by copyright laws which must be observed by all users. Each library has been supplied with a copy of the relevant Library Association poster which gives appropriate guidance. This should be displayed clearly near the PC.

Charging

1. Basic Use
   Access to the Internet through library PCs will be free to the public for the foreseeable future. This is being done in an attempt to generate maximum use and to allow us to get some months of experience of the service before making any final decisions. If a charge (by the hour, half hour etc.) is introduced eventually, it is very likely that certain groups will be entitled to a concessionary rate.

   Instructions on charging will be circulated before any charging system is introduced.

   NB Use of the Internet by staff, who consider it to be the most efficient way of answering a particular enquiry, will not attract a charge to the member of the public.
2. Prints
   All prints are charged at 10p per (A4) sheet. Staff should give out paper as requested, charging accordingly.
3. Floppy Disks
   Users are only able to download to floppy disk and these must be bought

from library staff at a charge of £0.50 per disk. Users are only allowed to use floppy disks bought from library staff at the time of each particular session. This is necessary in order to avoid the risk of viruses introduced by individual users' own disks.

4. Accounting for the income
   All income from sales of disks and from printing should be coded to 'Special Sales - Vatable'.

Bookings

In order to manage demand, especially while the service is free, a booking system operates at all libraries. Users may book sessions of ¼ hour, ½ hour or a full hour. Software is in place which will allow the PC to time out after the appropriate time has expired. Booking sessions will be forfeited if the user is over 15 minutes late and other users are waiting. Forms for the purpose of recording booked Internet sessions are available from your Group Headquarters. These include a space for the customer to sign that they agree to the Conditions of Use.

Retain these for the time being in case there are later queries concerning individuals not observing the conditions.

Where demand is heavy, any one individual may be limited to 1 hour's access per day.

Monitoring Use

Forms are provided on which to record the amount of use by the public, staff involvement etc. so that we can build up a picture of extra business and extra workloads. Please return these to the Public Services Librarian at Headquarters at the end of each month.

Public Instructions

Members of the public should be given information which instructs

- those with previous experience of Internet use to log on through Internet Explorer
- those with no previous experience to begin by accessing the BBC

WebWise program on CD-ROM which will be made available in all libraries.

(This option is not available at most libraries until more PCs are made available)

Publicity

At the moment, publicity takes the following forms –

1. A5 Flyers - intended to make communities (not just existing library users) aware of the service
2. Local promotions, e.g., targeting particular groups; taster sessions, supported by staff, at particular advertised times.

More permanent leaflets will be considered when the final form of the service is known.

Disability

Ways in which people with varying disabilities can make full use of the Internet facility are being investigated. These are likely to be implemented at a later date.

Children's Information Service

The first wave of PCs currently being implemented in our libraries has been financed entirely by the Department of Employment and Education through the Local Education Authority. This money has been used primarily to create a large number of access points throughout the County (not just in libraries) which allows the public to access the County's Children's Information Service on the World Wide Web. The Service gives the public details of all kinds of childcare facilities such as pre-school groups, nurseries, childminders etc. Every local authority in the country is being asked to create such a service.

Staff Involvement

1. All staff offer members of the public general guidance on how to access the Internet, how to access a particular site where the address (or URL) is known and the basic rudiments of searching via search engines. Staff are not expected to offer detailed training or lengthy support. This will be done by designated staff at formally arranged, pre-advertised sessions.

2. All library staff are responsible for ensuring that County Library policy on this service is observed by all users and for referring details of individuals who refuse to comply to their Group Librarian.

3. Information Librarians, under the direction of the Information Services Adviser, will help to build up a County list of useful sites which have been properly evaluated and can be recommended to the public.

4. Certain staff will use the Internet to answer enquiries from the public where this is the most effective way of dealing with an enquiry. Due to time restrictions on staff's ability to deal with such enquiries at local libraries, this will be done by librarians and also by library assistants who normally help staff reference enquiry points. Other staff should refer such enquiries to them.

Problems

This is a new service and the initial implementation at all of our libraries in quick succession has been very ambitious. Although the policy and the operational advice contained in these notes draw very heavily on the experience of other library services in both Britain and the United States of America, there will undoubtedly be situations and incidents which require further thought.

Any problems and concerns about the way in which we operate the service (other than those technical problems which go direct to the Help Desk) should be logged with the Public Services Librarian, via your Group Librarian, as they occur so that a countywide response can be given. Potentially, this is a very sensitive area of service and it is imperative that every library is observing exactly the same policy and is operating the service in an identical way.

Evaluation

Monitoring of these new services is ongoing.

The whole situation will be reviewed in terms of its success, the level of use, implications for purchase of printed materials, implications for staffing etc.

(Reproduced in anonymized form, by permission)

Appendix 4
Public policy documents

4.1 University of Derby, IT Code of Conduct
www.derby.ac.uk/computing-services/codeofconduct.
htm

Introduction

This Code of Conduct describes acceptable computer use at the University. The items in the code are not recommendations or guidelines but are University policy. This replaces all previous Codes of Conduct.

Breach of this I.T. Code of Conduct will lead to investigation and may lead to disciplinary action against the offender via existing disciplinary procedures. The University reserves the right, to report to the Police, any action/activity considered to be unlawful. Criminal proceedings may follow as a result.

Terms and Scope of the Document

1.1 Computer hardware or equipment, refers to that owned by the University irrespective as to its site. This includes microcomputers, networks, personal computers, laptops, workstations, minicomputers and multi-user systems, collectively called computer systems.

- This document applies to anyone who uses any of the University's computer systems or networks in any capacity.
- The I.T. Director is the Designated Authority within the University for all matters relating to the use of computer systems.

Complaints, Amendments and Exceptions

2.1 If you find libellous material on any of the University's computers systems, please report this immediately to the Company Secretary as well as to the Designated Authority.

2.2 If you believe that any of the guidance in this document has been broken please contact the Designated Authority, who will ensure that your concern is investigated.

2.3 If you have any suggestions for additions or amendments to this code then please contact the Designated Authority.

2.4 On occasions - as a user - you may need to access contentious materials or perform activities which may break these regulations. In such exceptional circumstances you must apply in writing to the Designated Authority (via your Course Leader, Head of Department or Dean) for permission BEFORE the activity takes place.

General Practice and Usage

3.1 The University's computer systems are to be used for teaching, study, research and administration purposes only. They must not be used for playing "computer games" or similar.

3.2 Any other use is subject to the permission of your manager or Dean.

3.3 In order to use the computing facilities, you must be authorised and/or registered; Computing Services is responsible for issuing usernames and passwords to authorised users.

3.4 Commercial or distribution activities are prohibited unless formally sanctioned by the University's Directorate.

3.5 Activities likely to damage the good name of the University are prohibited.

3.6 You must follow the Joint Academic Network (JANET) Acceptable Use Policy, http://www.ja.net/documents/use.html

3.7 You must respect the rights of others and conduct yourself in a quiet and orderly manner when using the computer systems. You must respect the published times for access to the facilities.

3.8 You may be required to show Computing Services personnel or Library and Learning Resources staff your ID card (as proof of identity). Please keep your ID card with you and be prepared to show it when asked. For example if you require any changes to be made to your network account you will have to produce your ID card.

Monitoring

4.1 If there is reasonable belief that any of the regulations in this document are being contravened, the Designated Authority may order the examination of any web pages, E-mail messages or network account data on any computer system owned by the University. In line with legal requirements and regulations, the Designated Authority also reserves the right to examine E-mails and other internet usage for the purpose of routine and necessary audits of computer archives/back-up tapes and to investigate suspected criminal activity. This would only be in circumstances where this is a legitimate business requirement and would be performed under controlled conditions, and as such would not be considered an infringement of an individual's Human Rights.

4.2 Computing Services reserves the right to inspect and validate any items of University owned computer equipment connected to the network.

4.3 Any other computer equipment connected to the University's network can be removed if it is deemed to be interfering with the operation of the network.

4.4 For security/legal purposes Computing Services may record and keep audit data generated when users access computer and other systems at the University.

4.5 The University reserves the right to report to the Police any action/activity considered to be unlawful.

Prohibitions

5.1 Internet/Network

5.1.1 You must not try to gain unauthorised access to any computer system anywhere using the University's computer systems; this is commonly called hacking. It is a criminal offence (Computer Misuse Act 1990) to gain unauthorised access to a computer system to make any unauthorised modification of computer material (including the introduction of a computer virus) or to interfere with any computing system provided in the interests of health and safety.

5.1.2 You must not allow unauthorised access to occur by your negligence.

5.1.3 You must not disseminate any information which enables others to gain unauthorised access to computer material (this includes instructions for gaining such access, computer codes or other devices which facilitate unauthorised access).

5.1.4 You must not disseminate any information which may lead to any unauthorised modification of computer materials (such modification would include activities such as the circulation of "infected" software or the unauthorised use of a password).

5.1.5 You must not disseminate any material which may incite or encourage others to carry out unauthorised access to or modification of computer materials.

5.1.6 You must not use the facilities in a way that restricts the services available to others e.g. deliberate or reckless overloading of access links or switching equipment.

5.1.7 When you use the University's computer system to gain access to remote sites it is your personal responsibility to ensure that only approved links are used. It is also your responsibility to ensure that your activities conform to the local regulations of the site.

5.1.8 You must not change the function or role of any system/network component within the University's network without the permission of the Designated Authority.

5.1.9 You must not set-up any network services (e.g. web servers, E-mail servers etc.) unless formally sanctioned by the Designated Authority.

5.1.10 You must not delete or amend the data or data structures of others without their permission.

5.1.11 You must not introduce any harmful or nuisance programs, files or macros (e.g. viruses, worms, Trojan horses) onto any computer system. You must not take any deliberate action to circumvent any precautions taken or prescribed to prevent this or cause any form of damage to any of the University's computer systems.

5.1.12 You must not register any domain name, which includes the name of the University, or any name which may mislead the public into believing that the domain name refers to the University.

5.1.13 The University is committed to the prevention of access to and publication through any of its computing services of any material that it may consider pornographic, violent or unlawful. Accordingly you must not generate, change, use, store, print or transmit information, programs or any other data that can reasonably be judged to be inappropriate or offensive to others. This includes material which is designed to or is likely to cause annoyance, inconvenience or needless anxiety, particularly if of a threatening nature or which is intended to harass, frighten, promote or encourage racism or any other discriminatory or offensive material.

5.1.14 You must not place links to sites which facilitate illegal or improper use, where copyright protected works, such as computer software, are unlawfully distributed or which display pornographic materials.

5.1.15 You must not place links to bulletin boards which are likely to publish defamatory materials or contain discriminatory statements.

5.2 Security

5.2.1 You must not let other people use your username. You must not reveal your password(s) or username to anybody. Passwords must adhere to accepted good password practice; advice about what constitutes a good password may be obtained from Computing Services' Help Desks or from http://www.derby.ac.uk/computing-services/password.html

5.2.2 You must not violate the privacy of others on the computer systems.

5.2.3 For your own security you must not leave your workstation "logged in" when unattended. Where practical, action will be taken against people who leave their station "logged in" and unattended.

5.3 E-mail

5.3.1 You must not send unwanted E-mail.

5.3.2 You must not post or send binary files to E-mail groups or other areas such as USENET groups.

5.3.3 You must not create or transmit chain letters, hoax virus warnings, pyramid letters or similar schemes using E-mail.

5.4 General

5.4.1 You must only use equipment (and mains leads) at the University that have been Portable Appliance Tested (PAT) by University approved staff. The equipment must also have an up-to-date green PAT-testing label attached to it.

5.4.2 You must not modify or delete files on the hard disks of the lab computers.

5.4.3 You must not interfere with the use by others of the computer systems. You must not remove or interfere with output belonging to others.

5.4.4 You must abide by the local rules for individual rooms or school-based computing facilities. Eating, drinking and smoking within computing laboratories are prohibited.

5.5 Web Pages

5.5.1 All official University web pages must conform to any stylistic or publishing guidelines produced by CEDM or Marketing.

5.5.2 Any "unofficial" web pages hosted on University web servers must not be linked directly to the University home page or linked directly to the school/department homepages. These pages must not include the University logo. Pages such as this should include a disclaimer stating, "The views and opinions expressed are those of the individual concerned and not necessarily those of the University".

Legal

6.1 The Data Protection Act 1998 regulates the storage of personal information (i.e. any information that can be identified as relating to a particular person or persons) on computer systems. Before storing any such information on the University computer system, you must notify the Designated Authority in writing. It is your responsibility to ensure that any such information complies with the law. For more details see http://www.dataprotection.gov.uk

6.2 Libel is a civil wrong which, in proven cases, may incur substantial compensation. It is very complicated and therefore one of the easiest laws to contravene through ignorance. Facts concerning individuals or organisations must be accurate and verifiable and views or opinions must not portray their subjects in any way that could damage their reputation. Check with the Company Secretary (x1098) before publicly displaying contentious material. IF IN DOUBT, DO NOT PUBLISH! Remember Web pages and E-mail messages may be regarded as publishing.

Copyright

7.1 The copyright laws of the UK and other countries must not be infringed. Downloading material from the Internet carries the risk of infringing copyright. This applies to files, documents and software, which must be licensed. Material illegally copied in this country or elsewhere and then transmitted to another country via the Internet, will also infringe the copyright laws of the country receiving it. Copyright, Designs and Patents Act 1988 is applicable to all types of creations, including text, graphics and sounds by an author or an artist. This will include any that are accessible through the University's computer systems. Any unloading or downloading of information through on-line technologies which is not authorised by the copyright owner will be deemed to be an infringement of her/his rights. You must not make, transmit or store an electronic copy of copyright material on the University's computing systems without the permission of the owner.

Software

8.1 Presenting a licence agreement to the Designated Authority will not be enough evidence to prove that you are entitled to install, copy or disseminate the software on any of the University's computer systems.

8.2 You must always comply with all valid regulations covering the use of software, whether those regulations are made by law, by the producer of the software, by the supplier of the software (e.g. CHEST) by the University or by any other legitimate authority. If you have any doubts contact the Designated Authority before using the software.

8.3 The University has the right to remove any unauthorised software from any of its computer systems.

8.4 The making, use and possession of any copy of computer software without the licence of the owner of the program is illegal, and may leave both you and the University open to legal proceedings. It is therefore of the utmost importance that you comply with all software licensing regulations and laws.

8.5 You must not install ANY third party software that is not licensed to the University on any of the University's computer systems under any circumstances.

8.6 Unlicensed copies of computer software must not be brought onto University premises, uploaded to or downloaded from University machinery, or passed across University networks.

8.7 If you are in any doubt as to whether computer software in your possession is held under a valid licence, it should not be used until you have verified that it is legal copy. In addition to a valid licence, evidence that the software was purchased through the University's finance system will also be required.

8.8 Computer software may not be copied for the purpose of student study, research or criticism without the written permission of the copyright owner.

8.9 You must not distribute, sell, hire or otherwise deal with any unauthorised copies of computer software.

8.10 Any of the University's schools or departments' senior managers may order regular unscheduled audits of selected computers systems within their school or department to ensure the legality of software installed or in use.

Liability, Warranty and Related Matters

9.1 The University will not be liable for any loss, damage or inconvenience arising directly or indirectly from the use of any facility provided. The University takes reasonable care to prevent corruption of information and strives to maintain effective security on all of its computer systems. However it cannot and does not give warranties about the integrity of information or about the security or confidentiality of data (including electronic mail) or other materials submitted or processed by the University or otherwise deposited or left in reception or other areas. It may be necessary on occasions for selected University staff to gain access to password protection information stored on the computer systems.

9.2 Neither the University nor any University employees or bodies will be held responsible for the correctness or otherwise of results produced by using its computer facilities.

9.3 While every reasonable endeavour is made to ensure that the computer systems are available as scheduled and function correctly, no liability whatsoever can be accepted by the Designated Authority for any loss or delay because of any equipment malfunction.

9.4 If as a result of misuse of the computer systems an individual causes the University to be involved in legal action, the University reserves its right to take consequential action against the said individual.

E-mail Guidelines

These guidelines should be read in conjunction with the above.

10.1 Recommendations/Good Practice

10.1.1 E-mail messages should not ordinarily be composed in capital letters, as this can be interpreted as 'shouting'.

10.1.2 Try and be familiar with general housekeeping 'good practice' and delete E-mail messages regularly.

10.1.3 E-mail messages, either internally or externally, are not guaranteed to be private and, therefore, sending a message by E-mail should have the same amount of consideration and care as writing a letter. Please use 'disclaimers' where appropriate. Do not use E-mail in circumstances where permanent records need to be kept. Advice given by E-mail has the same legal consequences as any other written advice.

10.1.4 Consider placing the text non-urgent in the subject box when the message is low priority.

10.1.5 If you put your signature at the end of your E-mail, ensure that it contains correct contact details and do not make it longer than six lines.

10.1.6 Use Groupwise rules to efficiently organise your incoming E-mail.

10.1.7 Try and keep E-mails as short as possible.

10.1.8 E-mails should not be used to completely replace other forms of communication.

10.2 Prohibitions

10.2.1 You must not send unwanted E-mail to other users. Users must not post or send binaries to E-mail groups or other areas such as local USENET groups.

10.2.2 You must not create or transmit chain letters, pyramid letters or similar schemes using E-mail.

10.2.3 You must not violate the privacy of other users on the computer systems.

10.2.4 You must not use the facilities in a way that restricts the services available to other users e.g. deliberate or reckless overloading of access links or switching equipment.

10.2.5 You must not create or transmit material that infringes the copyright of another person or institution.

10.2.6 You must not attach inappropriate material such as pornography to outgoing E-mails. The internal recipient of any inappropriate material must bring the matter to the attention of the Designated Authority.

10.2.7 Messages must not include defamatory, libellous or sexually harassing statements or offensive comments based on gender, age, sexuality, race, disability or appearance.

10.2.8 You must not falsify or attempt to falsify E-mails to make them appear to have been originated from someone else or to provide false information where senders' details are required or sought.

10.3 General

10.3.1 You must take all reasonable care to ensure that data sent is 'virus free'.

10.3.2 Do NOT pass on virus warnings to anybody unless you are sure that that they are not a hoax. Please check at one of the following sites first

http://www.datafellows.com/virus-info/hoax/
http:/vil.mcafee.com/hoax.asp
http://urbanlegends.about.com/c/ht/00/07/How_Spot_Email_
  Hoax0962932962.htm

10.3.3 No E-mail system is 100% reliable: do not rely on E-mail as the only means of communicating important messages.

10.3.4 Remember, E-mail can be used as court evidence and an agreement by E-mail can create a binding contract.

Disciplinary Action

11.1 Breach of this I.T. Code of Conduct will lead to investigation and may lead to disciplinary action against the offender via existing disciplinary procedures. The University reserves the right to report to the Police, any action/activity considered to be unlawful. Criminal proceedings may follow as a result.

(Reproduced by permission of the University of Derby)

4.2 Loughborough University, Acceptable Use Policy

www.lboro.ac.uk/computing/info/policies/loughborough_aup.html

Computing/IT Acceptable Use Policy

The University seeks to promote and facilitate the proper and extensive use of computing/IT in the interests of learning and research. Whilst the traditions of academic freedom will be fully respected, this also requires responsible and legal use of the technologies and facilities made available to students and staff of the University.

This Acceptable Use Policy is intended to provide a framework for such use of Loughborough University's computing/IT resources. It applies to all computing and networking facilities provided by any department or section of the University. It should be interpreted such that it has the widest application, in particular references to Computing Services should, where appropriate, be taken to include departmental or other system managers responsible for the provision of a computing service.

The Acceptable Use Policy is taken to include the JANET Acceptable Use Policy published by the United Kingdom Educational and Research Network Association (UKERNA) and the Combined Higher Education Software Team (CHEST) Code of Conduct, together with its associated Copyright Acknowledgement. Members of the University and all other users of the University's facilities are bound by the provisions of these policies in addition to this Acceptable Use Policy.

1) Purpose of Use

University computing resources are provided to facilitate a person's work as an employee or student of the University, specifically for educational, training, administrative or research purposes.

Use for other purposes, such as personal electronic mail or recreational use of the World Wide Web or Usenet News, is a withdrawable privilege not a right. Any such use must not interfere with the user's duties or studies or any other person's use of computer systems and must not, in any way, bring the University into disrepute. Priority must always be granted to those needing facilities for academic work.

Commercial work for outside bodies, using centrally managed services requires explicit permission from the Director of Computing Services; such use, whether or not authorised, may be liable to charge.

2) Authorisation

In order to use the computing facilities of Loughborough University a person must first be authorised. Registration of all monthly salaried employees and registered students is carried out automatically. Other members of the University should apply to Computing Services for registration. Registration to use University services implies and is conditional upon acceptance of this Acceptable Use Policy, for which a signature of acceptance is required on joining the University.

The registration procedure grants authorisation to use the core facilities of the University. Following registration, a username and password will be allocated. Registration for other services may be requested by application to Computing Services.

All individually allocated usernames and passwords are for the exclusive use of the individual to whom they are allocated. The user is personally responsible and accountable for all activities carried out under their username. The password associated with a particular personal username must not be divulged to another person, except to trusted members of IT staff. Attempts to access or use any username, which is not authorised to the user, are prohibited. No-one may use, or attempt to use, computing resources allocated to another person, except when authorised by the provider of those resources.

All users must correctly identify themselves at all times. A user must not masquerade as another, withhold his/her identity or tamper with audit trails. A user should take all reasonable precautions to protect their resources. In particular, passwords used must adhere to accepted good password practice. Advice on what constitutes a good password may be obtained from Computing Services Web pages.

3) Privacy

It should be noted that systems staff, who have appropriate privileges, have the ability to access all files, including electronic mail files, stored on a computer which they manage.

Access to staff files will not normally be given to another member of staff unless authorised by the Director of Computing Services, who will use his/her discretion in consultation with a senior officer of the University, if appropriate. In such circumstances the Head of Department or Section, or more senior line manager, will be informed, and will normally be consulted prior to action being taken. Such access will normally only be granted where a breach of the law or this policy is suspected.

Student privacy is seen by the University as a privilege and not a right, hence students should not expect to hold or pass information, which they would not wish to be seen by members of staff. Systems staff are authorised to release the contents of a student's files to any member of staff who has a work-based reason for requiring this access.

Files, which are left behind after a student or member of staff leaves the University, will be considered to be the property of the University.

4) Behaviour

No person shall jeopardise the integrity, performance or reliability of computer equipment, software, data and other stored information. The integrity of the University's computer systems is jeopardised if users do not take adequate precautions against malicious software, such as computer virus programs. Reasonable care should also be taken to ensure that resource use does not result in a denial of service to others.

Conventional norms of behaviour apply to computer based information technology just as they would apply to more traditional media. Within the University setting this should also be taken to mean that the traditions of academic freedom will always be respected. The University, as expressed in its Equal Opportunities Policy, is committed to achieving an educational and working environment which provides equality of opportunity, and freedom from discrimination on the grounds of race, religion, sex, class, sexual orientation, age, disability or special need.

Distributing material, which is offensive, obscene or abusive, may be illegal and may also contravene University codes on harassment. Users of University computer systems must make themselves familiar with, and comply with, the University codes concerning all forms of harassment.

No user shall interfere or attempt to interfere in any way with information belonging to or material prepared by another user. Similarly no user shall make unauthorised copies of information belonging to another user. The same conventions of privacy should apply to electronically held information as to that held on traditional media such as paper.

For specific services the University may provide more detailed guidelines. In particular, users providing information on the World Wide Web must follow the University's Code of Practice for Online Publications, in addition to the policies provided in this Acceptable Use Policy. Users of services external to the University are expected to abide by any rules and codes of conduct applying to such services.

5) Definitions of Acceptable & Unacceptable Usage

Unacceptable use of University computers and network resources may be summarised as:

- the retention or propagation of material that is offensive, obscene or indecent, except in the course of recognised research or teaching that is permitted under UK and international law;
- propagation will normally be considered to be a much more serious offence;
- causing annoyance, inconvenience or needless anxiety to others, as specified in the JANET Acceptable Use Policy;
- defamation (genuine scholarly criticism is permitted);
- intellectual property rights infringement, including copyright, trademark, patent, design and moral rights;
- unsolicited advertising, often referred to as "spamming";
- attempts to break into or damage computer systems or data held thereon;
- attempts to access or actions intended to facilitate access to computers for which the individual is not authorised
- unauthorised resale of University or JANET services or information

These restrictions should be taken to mean, for example, that the following activities will normally be considered to be a breach of this policy:

- the distribution or storage by any means of pirated software
- non-academic activities which generate heavy network traffic, especially

those which interfere with others' legitimate use of IT services or which incur financial costs

- frivolous use of University owned Computer laboratories, especially where such activities interfere with others' legitimate use of IT services
- the deliberate viewing and/or printing of pornographic images the passing on of electronic chain mail
- the use of departmental academic mailing lists for non-academic purposes
- the purchase of blank CDs for the purpose of copying unlicensed copyright software
- the use of other people's web site material without the express permission of the copyright holder.

Other uses may be unacceptable in certain circumstances. In particular, users of the Student Hall Service should take account of the particular conditions of use applying to that service. It should be noted that Hall Service users should not provide any services to others via remote access. The installed machine on each network socket must be a workstation only and not provide any server-based services, including, but not limited to, Web, FTP, IRC, Streaming Media or email services.

It should be noted that individuals may be held responsible for the retention of attachment material that they have received, via electronic mail that they have read, but have never viewed.

Acceptable uses may include: personal email and recreational use of Internet services, as long as these are in keeping with the framework defined in this policy document and do not interfere with one's duties, studies or the work of others; and advertising via electronic notice boards, intended for this purpose, or via other University approved mechanisms. However such use must be regarded as a privilege and not as a right and may be withdrawn if abused or if the user is subject to a disciplinary procedure.

6) Legal Constraints

Any software and/or hard copy of data or information which is not generated by the user personally and which may become available through the use of University computing or communications resources shall not be copied or used without permission of the University or the copyright owner. In particular, it is up to the user to check the terms and conditions of any licence for the use of the software or information and to abide by them. Software and/or information provided by the University may only be used as part of the user's duties as an employee or student of the University or for educational purposes. The user agrees to abide by all the licensing agreements for software entered into by the University with other parties.

In the case of private work and other personal use of computing facilities, the University will not accept any liability for loss, damage, injury or expense that may result.

The user undertakes to comply with the provisions of the following Acts of Parliament (or any re-enactment thereof): Computer Misuse Act 1990, Criminal Justice and Public Order Act 1994, Copyright, Designs and Patents Act 1988, Trade Marks Act 1994, Data Protection Act 1984, Data Protection Act 1998; as well as all other relevant legislation and legal precedent. See below for a summary of the main points. Copies of these documents are available through the University Library. Further advice should be obtained through the Director of Computing Services in the first instance.

Computer Misuse Act 1990

This Act makes it an offence

- to erase or amend data or programs without authority
- to obtain unauthorised access to a computer
- to "eavesdrop" on a computer
- to make unauthorised use of computer time or facilities maliciously
- to corrupt or erase data or programs
- to deny access to authorised users.

Criminal Justice & Public Order Act 1994

This defines a criminal offence of intentional harassment, which covers all forms of harassment, including sexual. A person is guilty of an offence if, with intent to cause a person harassment, alarm or distress, s/he:-

- uses threatening, abusive or insulting words or behaviour, or disorderly behaviour; or
- displays any writing, sign or other visible representation which is

threatening, abusive or insulting, thereby causing that or another person harassment, alarm or distress.

Copyright, Designs and Patents Act 1988

This Act, together with a number of Statutory Instruments that have amended and extended it, controls copyright law. It makes it an offence to copy all, or a substantial part, which can be a quite small portion, of a copyright work. There are, however, certain limited user permissions, such as fair dealing, which means under certain circumstances permission is not needed to copy small amounts for research or private study. The Act also provides for Moral Rights, whereby authors can sue if their name is not included in a work they wrote, or if the work has been amended in such a way to impugn their reputation. Copyright covers materials in print and electronic form, and includes words, images, sound, moving images, TV broadcasts and many other media.

Trade Marks Act 1994

This Act provides protection for Registered Trade Marks, which can be any symbol (words or images) or even shapes of objects that are associated with a particular set of goods or services. Anyone who uses a Registered Trade Mark without permission can be sued. They can also be sued if they use a Mark that is confusingly similar to an existing Mark.

Data Protection Acts 1984 and 1998

The 1984 Act requires that any person or organisation processing information about individuals in machine-readable form must register with the Data Protection Registrar and must abide by a number of principles. It also gives individuals the right to inspect information held about them, to demand amendments to records if they are inaccurate, and to sue if they suffer financial damage as a result of incorrect information. When the 1998 Act is brought fully into force in 2000 it will repeal the 1984 Act. It will extend the provisions to material in manual form, and place the onus in many cases on the person or organisation handling the personal information to request permission from the individuals before using the information.

7) University Discipline

Staff or students who break this Acceptable Use Policy will find themselves subject to the University's disciplinary procedures and may be subject to criminal proceedings. The University reserves its right to take legal action against individuals who cause it to be involved in legal proceedings as a result of their violation of licensing agreements and/or other contraventions of this policy.

8) Policy Supervision and Advice

The responsibility for the supervision of this Acceptable Use Policy is delegated to Computing Services. A senior member of Computing Services, normally the Assistant Director (Customer Services) or their nominee, will be designated as the person responsible for the day to day management of the policy's enforcement. He/she will liaise with the Director of Computing Services, the University Librarian, the Security Manager, the Copyright Officer, the Intellectual Property Co-ordinator, the Registrar and Heads of Department as required. Procedural guidelines will be published from time to time as a separate document.

Any suspected breach of this policy should be reported to a member of Computing Services staff. The responsible senior member will then take the appropriate action within the University's disciplinary framework, in conjunction with other relevant branches of the University. Computing Services staff will also take action when infringements are detected in the course of their normal duties. Actions will include, where relevant, immediate removal from online information systems of material that is believed to infringe the law. The University reserves the right to audit and/or suspend without notice any account pending any enquiry.

This policy is not exhaustive and inevitably new social and technical developments will lead to further uses which are not fully covered. In the first instance students should address questions concerning what is acceptable to their supervisor; staff should initially contact their departmental IT Acceptable Use Policy Adviser or Head of Department/Section. Where there is any doubt the matter should be raised with Computing Services, whose staff will ensure that all such questions are dealt with at the appropriate level within the University.

(Reproduced by permission of Loughborough University)

4.3 Leeds City Council, Leeds Library and Information Service Public Internet Access Policy

- Leeds Library & information Service provides public access to the Internet in keeping with its role as a source of information, intellectual development, and enrichment for the community. Internet access is not filtered except in Children's Libraries, users are responsible for the materials accessed. Leeds Library & Information Service has no control over the information accessed and cannot be held responsible for the content or quality of the information retrieved.

- Users must not attempt to introduce any virus or similar malicious code. Leeds Library and Information Service take every precaution to protect these terminals from viruses, but accept no responsibility for any damage caused to files.

- No responsibility can be accepted for any financial loss incurred through transactions undertaken on these terminals.

- Transmission of any material in violation of any laws is prohibited. This includes, but is not limited to: copyrighted material, threatening or obscene material, pornographic material, or material protected by trade secret. Use for any commercial purpose is also prohibited.

- Any unacceptable use will result in access being withdrawn, this includes any attempts to alter the set-up or configuration of the computer or using their own software or disks.

- As is the case with all other library materials, any restriction of a child's access to the Internet is the responsibility of the child's parent or legal guardian.

- Due to our limited resources, we reserve the right to restrict Internet access to research and information sources only.

- All members of the public will be asked to produce a Leeds Library and Information Service membership card at the time of accessing the Internet on public terminals.

I have read and understood the terms & conditions set out above and agree

Signature..

Name (print)......................................   Date...........................

Leeds Library and Information Service Membership Number.....................

Home postcode/country...........................

4.4 Dublin City Public Libraries, Acceptable Usage Policy
www.iol.ie/dublincitylibrary/internet.htm

Dublin City Public Libraries aim to inform, enrich, empower and extend individual life-chances through the provision of information, ideas, resources and programmes which bring to local communities the benefits of global thought, life-long learning experience and diversity of heritage and culture.

Dublin City Public Libraries acknowledges its role as an important participant in government initiatives to develop the Information Society, to combat disadvantage and to promote equality of access and opportunity.

The availability of Free Public Internet Access complements and extends traditional library service provision. The following conditions apply:

1 Users must be aware that the World Wide Web is an unregulated information network, enabling access to ideas, information and images. Users are required to be responsible in their use of the World Wide Web.

2 Free Internet-based computer reference facilities are available to all registered members of Dublin City Public Libraries. Membership is open to residents, students, visitors and people working in the city. Full details are available on request.

3 Adults who are not eligible for membership as outlined above may obtain special membership for access to Internet-based computer reference services on production of satisfactory proof of personal Identity.

4 Dublin City Public Libraries cannot guarantee the accuracy of information on the World Wide Web, nor can they accept responsibility for, or supervise content which may be accessed inadvertently or otherwise by a user. The library accepts no responsibility for damage, loss, costs or expenses arising either directly or indirectly from use of the library's free Internet based computer reference services.

5 Users may register with any of the free e-mail address services. However, inappropriate mail must not be sent or received. Dublin City Public Libraries cannot accept responsibility for any communication received or sent by personal e-mail account holders.

6 Parents and guardians are obliged to take responsibility for their children's use of the web. Children under the age of 12 are welcome to use the Internet-based computer facilities:

- provided they are accompanied by a parent or guardian or teacher, or they are supervised or directed by a teacher or other responsible adult over the age of 18.
7 Secondary school children under the age of 15 are welcome to use the Internet-based computer facilities:
   - provided they are accompanied by a parent or guardian or they are supervised or directed by a teacher or other responsible adult over the age of 18.
   - Or provided a parent or guardian authorises such use in writing by signing Permission Forms in the presence of library staff.
8 The use of chat room facilities is not permitted.
9 Software is in place which inhibits the accessing of designated illegal and inappropriate sites. A Management system delivers specific data related to each personal computer. This system produces a detailed activity log, which can be used to analyse citywide usage patterns, or if required, by library, by groups of users or by individual users. This information will be monitored on an ongoing basis. The library reserves the right to terminate an Internet session at any time.
10 Users may not create, access, copy, store, transmit, download or publish any material which
   - Is obscene, racist, defamatory or illegal
   - Causes harassment or gross offence to others
   - Constitutes a breach of copyright laws or licensing agreements.
11 Users may not:
   - Use the library's workstations as a staging ground to gain unauthorised access to the library's networks or computer systems or to any other network or computer system
   - Obstruct the work of others by consuming large amounts of system resources or by deliberately crashing any library computer system
   - Make any attempt to damage computer equipment or software
   - Make any attempt to alter software configurations in a malicious manner
   - Make any attempt to cause degradation of system performance
   - Use any library workstation for illegal or criminal purpose.
12 In the interest of equality and fairness and in order to ensure the effective use of library resources, users must abide by booking procedures and

operational arrangements in force at branch libraries.

13 Users who wish to appeal decisions relating to the above policy and procedures should do so in writing to the Dublin City Librarian.

14 All users are required to indicate their compliance with the library's Acceptable Use Policy before access will be facilitated.

Contact your local branch to find out times of availability and locations. Details can be found here of individual branches.

(Reproduced by permission of Dublin City Public Libraries)

4.5 Anytown Secondary School, Responsible Internet Use
www.kented.org.uk/ngfl/policy/secondary.html

Rules for Staff and Students

The school computer system provides Internet access to students and staff. This Responsible Internet Use statement will help protect students, staff and the school by clearly stating what is acceptable and what is not.

- Access must only be made via the user's authorised account and password, which must not be given to any other person.
- School computer and Internet use must be appropriate to the student's education or to staff professional activity.
- Copyright and intellectual property rights must be respected.
- Users are responsible for e-mail they send and for contacts made.
- E-mail should be written carefully and politely. As messages may be forwarded, e-mail is best regarded as public property.
- Anonymous messages and chain letters must not be sent.
- The use of public chat rooms is not allowed.
- The school ICT systems may not be used for private purposes, unless the headteacher has given permission for that use.
- Use for personal financial gain, gambling, political purposes or advertising is forbidden.
- The security of ICT systems must not be compromised, whether owned by the school or by other organisations or individuals.
- Irresponsible use may result in the loss of Internet access.

The school may exercise its right by electronic means to monitor the use of the school's computer systems, including the monitoring of web-sites, the interception of E-mails and the deletion of inappropriate materials in circumstances where it believes unauthorised use of the school's computer system is or may be taking place, or the system is or may be being used for criminal purposes or for storing text or imagery which is unauthorised or unlawful.

(Template reproduced from copyright materials made available
for educational use by Kent County Council)

4.6 Invicta Primary School, Responsible Internet Use

www.kented.org.uk/ngfl/policy/primary.html

We use the school computers and Internet connection for learning.
    These rules will help us to be fair to others and keep everyone safe.

- I will ask permission before entering any Web site, unless my teacher has already approved that site.
- On a network, I will use only my own login and password, which I will keep secret.
- I will not look at or delete other people's files.
- I will not bring floppy disks into school without permission.
- I will only e-mail people I know, or my teacher has approved.
- The messages I send will be polite and sensible.
- When sending e-mail, I will not give my home address or phone number, or arrange to meet someone.
- I will ask for permission before opening an e-mail or an e-mail attachment sent by someone I do not know.
- I will not use Internet chat.
- I see anything I am unhappy with or I receive messages I do not like, I will tell a teacher immediately.
- I know that the school may check my computer files and may monitor the Internet sites I visit.
- I understand that if I deliberately break these rules, I could be stopped from using the Internet or computers.

The school may exercise its right by electronic means to monitor the use of the school's computer systems, including the monitoring of web-sites, the interception of E-mail and the deletion of inappropriate materials in circumstances where it believes unauthorised use of the school's computer system is or may be taking place, or the system is or may be being used for criminal purposes or for storing text or imagery which is unauthorised or unlawful.

(Template reproduced from copyright materials made available
for educational use by Kent County Council)

Appendix 5
Council of Europe Guidelines

Public Access and Freedom of Expression in Networked Information: Guidelines for a European Cultural Policy
culture.coe.fr/postsummit/nti/en/documents/helsinki/guidelines.htm

1. Principles of Public Access

1.1 Cultural institutions providing public access to networked information and communication should do so for all, without regard to race, nationality, religion, culture, political affiliation, physical or learning impairment, gender or sexual orientation.

1.2 It is the responsibility of individuals using Public Access Points to decide for themselves what they should, or should not, access.

1.3 Those providing Public Access Points should respect the privacy of users and treat knowledge of what they have accessed or wish to access as confidential.

1.4 So as to enable users to make the fullest and most independent use possible of networked information and communication, those providing Public Access Points should provide assistance for everyone to acquire the skills required to use such services.

1.5 In the interests of an informed citizenry and a healthy democratic process, access to information content generated by local, regional and national public authorities should be promoted at all Public Access Points.

2. Children's Access

2.1 Children choosing to use those Public Access Points that are provided for whole community use should, as far as possible, be able to do so under the same conditions as other users. Nevertheless, in order to avoid access to harmful and/or illegal content, filtering systems requesting the use of personal age codes should be provided at Public Access Points.

2.2 Children have a right to expect that Public Access Points will provide instruction and assistance in developing those skills which will enable them to become confident and capable users.

2.3 Although it is the responsibility of parents to advise their children about choices in the use of networked information and communication, the staff of Public Access Points should provide guidance for children.

2.4 Because networks offer real time communication as well as access to stored information, parents should take particular trouble to advise their children about the potential risks of online contacts made with strangers. Parental warnings about online contact with strangers should be reinforced as part of the education and training processes.

2.5 Access points provided specifically for children should provide them with high levels of guidance and assistance in locating content appropriate to their needs.

3. Access in Specialised Institutions

3.1 Specialised institutions such as museums, archives and subject-oriented information centres have a particular responsibility to promote access to content in their fields by developing new information resources and programmes to digitise relevant existing resources.

3.2 Unlike cultural institutions which are set up to serve the whole community with a full range of information, it may be necessary for specialised institutions to develop a policy which confines the permitted range of access to that which is relevant to the institution's aims and objectives. Additionally, institutions operating intranets and closed access internets, will need to restrict access to material such as that, in the case of archives, relating to certain aspects of official administration and personal data. Users should be made aware of any such restrictions by the public display of the relevant policy statements.

3.3 Specialised institutions should not, however, impose limitations beyond the extent needed to ensure resources are committed to their primary purposes.

4. Management of Public Access Points

4.1 A Public Access Point is more than a group of workstations with network connection: a properly managed environment with suitable levels and quality of staffing is also required.

4.2 Those responsible for the education and training of information professionals should ensure that the programmes they provide contain elements designed to produce well-prepared managers and staff for Public Access Points.

4.3 It is the responsibility of management and staff of Public Access Points to facilitate public access to networked information and communication so that individual users have the necessary skills and a suitable environment in which to make their choices of information sources and services freely and confidently.

4.4 The staff of Public Access Points should be pro-active in identifying and facilitating access to quality networked information content, particularly for young people. It is appropriate for information professionals to create gateway pages for this purpose.

5. Disruptive Use

5.1 It is the responsibility of the managers and staff of Public Access Points to provide a positive and encouraging atmosphere for the use of networked information and communication. This may, in turn, require them to deal with instances of access to content by one user that disrupts the work of others.

5.2 Staff should not be required to exercise general supervision of usage with the express intention of identifying the use of illegal or otherwise distasteful content. However, if such use is drawn to their attention, they have an obligation to request the cessation of illegal use and to encourage more discreet use of other disturbing content.

5.3 Cases in which it proves necessary to request a user to discontinue access to particular content should be handled according to a pre-established and transparent process.

5.4 In such cases the action taken should be reviewed immediately to establish whether it was appropriate and what further action, including restoring the user's right of access, might be required.

5.5 The layout and equipment of Public Access Points should be designed so as to minimise disturbance from images and sounds retrieved by other users.

6. Filtering, Rating and Warning Pages

6.1 The use by the managers of Public Access Points of software filtering systems to block access to certain content is an unwarranted interference with the individual's freedom of access to information. If filtering and blocking systems are to be made available, it should only be as an option that individuals can choose and calibrate at their own preferred levels.

6.2 The use of software products (known as recommender systems, intelligent agents, content management systems, etc.) to filter networked content for positive recommendations is potentially an important contribution to effective network use and the availability of such products at Public Access Points is to be encouraged.

6.3 Metadata attached to content, which might include rating or labelling, can be used to help users make selections, and it can also facilitate recommendation of content by suitable software on grounds of quality and relevance.

6.4 Rating data which is applied to a site, whether by the information providers themselves or by independent third party agencies, should conform to standards created by independent bodies recognised by information providers as competent to perform this task. An appropriate metadata platform should be used for such purposes.

6.5 When assisting users, the staff of Public Access Points should be prepared to draw their attention to the warning pages attached to many sites that contain controversial content, but should also make it clear that not all such sites carry warning pages.

6.6 The age verification systems attached to some sites with controversial content also warn users that they might wish to avoid such content, but users should be made aware of the risks associated with supplying personal data to such systems if they are not operated by reputable organisations.

7. Internet Use Policies

7.1 A Public Access Point should be operated within a clearly articulated and publicly available policy, consistent with the principles of this text, and expressing the balance of responsibilities between staff and users.

7.2 The management of Public Access Points should involve relevant bodies from civil society (professional associations, network management boards, trades associations, local community groups, library advisory boards, school parent/teacher associations, etc.) when discussing policy on access and developing Internet Use Policy documents for public distribution and display.

7.3 Guidance in the formation of policy should be sought from the large numbers of existing Internet Use Policies, acceptable use policies, parental guidelines, and codifications of 'netiquette'.

7.4 The application of policy in practice should be subject to constant review and consultation so that the aims and objectives of the service continue to be achieved.

(Extracted from Council of Europe Publishing publication
of the same title, ISBN 92-871-4651-1, by permission)

Index